YESHIVATH BETH MOSHE OF SCRANTON is proud of its
many contributions to Torah scholarship. Since its
beginning in 1965, the Scranton Yeshiva has elevated
the calibre of Torah education through its high school,
beis medrash and Kollel – Graduate Program.

Our alumni rank among the leading Torah educators
and lay leaders in America.

Over the years, dissemination of valuable, informative
and spiritually uplifting Jewish literature has become a
tradition at Beth Moshe. It is in this tradition that we
present with pride this current volume.

לקוטי תפלות

A Selection of Psalms for
Livelihood, Gratitude and Repentance

A Time for
Prayer

YESHIVATH BETH MOSHE

Typesetting:
Star Composition/N.Y.C.
15M080195BCPC
ISBN: 0-9626226-7-2

Printed in the United States of America

Preface

Whether we realize it or not, prayer is a powerful instrument. The efficaciousness of prayer is so clear, that the Rambam states that anyone who fails to pray for fellow Jews in times of trouble is guilty - not of apathy - but of cruelty.

But prayer is not limited merely to troubled times. The very air we breath and the bread we eat are gifts from the Almighty. Our being ever cognizant of these gifts - the gifts of life itself - will, in turn, guide us to beseech Hashem for His benevolence and will spur us to show our gratitude to Him. And if, God forbid, we at times err or go astray, we know from Hashem Himself - through the Torah and our prophets - that even then we can beseech Hashem for his forgiveness.

However, oft times we are at a loss of the proper words to beg forgiveness or plead for sustenance. But our sages did not fail us in this plight, and especially King David in his divinely inspired wisdom has given us just the right words to express our humble entreaty.

But so often, even after our entreaties have been answered favorably, many of us fail to show our gratitude to Hashem for his benevolence. The classic illustration concerns the man who falls from a cliff, screams out, "Hashem, save me!.....Never mind, Hashem, I just caught on to a branch." It is incumbent upon us to show our gratitude for all the many wonderful things Hashem does for us. But again, we are often at a loss for the proper words. And, again, the Psalmist, with his lofty neshoma, shows us the way.

As in the past, where we published the warmly accepted book of prayers, "In Time of Need", Yeshiva Beth Moshe deems it a privilege once again to carefully present a selection of the appropriate Psalms to ask for Hashem's sustenance, to beg His forgiveness, and to show gratitude for his bountiful goodness.

It is our hope that the Jewish public will use this volume to bring all our people closer to Hashem through fervent prayer and a deeper appreciation of our historic ability to communicate with our Creator.

We wish to acknowledge Mrs. Rivka Walkin, Mrs. Esther Flam and Rochel Flam for all their help in typing, editing and proofreading this book.

Our heartfelt thanks to Reb Yankel Weiss of Star Composition for all his help and expertise in typesetting this book. He is always a pleasure to work with.

Rabbi Chaim Bressler
Rabbi Yaakov Schnaidman
Tammuz, 5756

TABLE OF CONTENTS

פתיחה לאמירת תהילים

אמירת תהלים בכל יום או בעת שמחה או על כל צרה שלא
תבא מקובלת לנו מדורי דורות. ואבותינו שמסרו לנו הנהגה זו ידעו
התועלת ותיקון הגדול הבא על ידי אמירתו, ועליהם אנו סומכים.
ומכל מקום לפי ערכנו נראה לבאר המעלה הגדולה באמירת
תהלים.

מי שאומר תהלים בכוונה הראויה, ומכוין פירוש המלות
כפשוטן, הרי בעת שמחה הוא נותן שבח והודאה להקב״ה על כל
הטוב שעשה עמו. ובעת צרה ח״ו משים בטחונו רק בהקב״ה שהוא
מלא חסד ורחמים ובידו להושיעו מהצרה. ועל ידי אמירתן בכל
יום ויום הוא סומך על הקב״ה ואינו זז מהאמונה החזקה שהקב״ה
הוא הפועל ישועות ומצמיח גאולות.

יסוד הישועות ושורש הגאולות הוא על ידי האמונה בהקב״ה
שמאמין שהכל תחת ידו, וכל מה שאירע לנו הוא בהשגחה
מדוייקת ולהאמין שאין לרחמיו וחסדיו גבול, אמירת תהלים הוא
קיום אמונה זאת.

עוד ידוע לנו מאבותינו שיש סודות נפלאים באמירת תהלים.
רוב ההמון ובפרט בדורות שלנו אינם מכוונים לאלו הסודות. ומ״מ
יש כוונה כוללת בעת אמירתו וחשובה כאלו כיוון להסודות. והוא
שהאדם יקבל על עצמו שרצונו הוא לעשות נחת רוח ליוצרו
ובאמירתן היא מקיים רצון קונו. ועל ידי כוונה זו כל התיקונים
השייכים לאותיות ותיבות היוצאים מפיו יפעלו פעולתם להביא
עלינו ברכה מלמעלה. הקב״ה יסייענו להיות מן אותם העובדים
באופן הנרצה.

Introduction

Recitation of Tehillim daily, or at times of joy or trouble, has been an accepted tradition for generations. Our forefathers, who passed on this tradition to us, knew the benefits and great spiritual improvement which comes through its recitation. And while we are justified in simply relying upon these forefathers, we can nevertheless attempt to clarify the great benefit derived from reciting Tehillim.

Whoever says Tehillim with proper intention – namely to contemplate the simple meaning of the words – will give praise and thanks to God during happy times, for all the benevolence He has granted. And during troubled times, God forbid – he will put his trust in the Holy One Blessed be He, Who is full of mercy and compassion, Who comes to the rescue. He will praise Hashem each day for the wonders of Creation. Thus every day of one's life – no matter what the circumstances – he will rely on God with the unwavering faith that He is the great Savior and Redeemer.

Faith in Hashem (that everything is in His hands and that all that happens to us is with precise Divine direction) and the belief in His unlimited compassion and mercy is the basis of salvation and the root of redemption. He is the Redeemer, the Healer, the Savior. Reciting of Tehillim is the fulfillment of this faith.

Furthermore, we know from our forefathers that there are wondrous hidden meanings in the Tehillim. The vast population – particularly in our times – do not know these hidden meanings. Yet, if we say the Psalms with proper fervor, it is considered as though we said the Tehillim with their concealed meanings. How does one do this? The person saying the Tehillim simply accepts upon himself to bring – as it were – satisfaction to the Creator, fully realizing that this is the will and the true service of Hashem. With these lofty thoughts, all the spiritual enhancement possible to come from the Psalmist's words will take effect, and bestow blessings from above. May we be granted God's help to be among those who serve in this most acceptable manner.

– 1 –

Tehillim for Livelihood

כוונות נכבדות למתפלל על פרנסה

1) יכון שהעולם נברא עם מדת החסד, והקב"ה משגיח בהעולם ליתן לכל חי פרנסתו וזה מבואר בקרא פותח את ידך ומשביע לכל חי רצון. ועוד כתיב נותן לחם לכל בשר כי לעולם חסדו.

2) צריך להאמין דאין השתדלות האדם סיבה לפרנסתו, דבאמת הקב"ה הוא המפרנס, והניחו צנצנת המן לדורות להראות אמיתית ענין זה. ומ"מ מוטל על האדם להשתדל בשביל פרנסתו דכך גזרה חכמתו דבאופן זה ישפיע לאדם. והוא מנסיונות עוה"ז, דהאדם צריך להשתדל אבל עם כל זה לא יחשוב דהשתדלותו הוי סיבה.

3) לא יפול ברשת מחשבת בנ"א שיש לאדם אחר כח ליטול או ליתן לו פרנסתו. דסיבה אמיתיית לפרנסתו הוא הקב"ה.

4) מעלה גדולה שיתפלל בכל יום לפרנסתו ולקבוע בלבו ענינים אלו, ותפלתו מועלת הרבה. ויחשוב דתפלתו עיקרת והשתדלותו טפלה, וכן מבואר בקרא ודורשי ה' לא יחסרו כל טוב.

5) מדת החסד הוא בלי שיעור וכמו שרואין זרע קטן יש בכחו להצמיח אילן גדול. ואם נראה לאדם שפרנסתו הוי כהר גדול, ואיך יכול להשיג מה שהוא צריך, יתחזק באמונה דמדת החסד הוא בלי גבול.

THOUGHTS BEFORE PRAYING FOR LIVELIHOOD

1) The world was created with the attribute of loving kindness and Hashem personally analyzes the world in order to give everyone his sustenance. This is stated in the verse "*You open Your hand and sate all living things its needs.*" and in the verse "*He gives bread to all flesh for His loving kindness endures forever.*"

2) One must not believe that ones own toil is the source of his livelihood, rather Hashem is his provider. Hashem commanded Moshe to set aside a portion of Manna to be saved for future generations to teach us this lesson. Nevertheless one is obligated to toil for a livelihood because this is what Hashem in His infinite wisdom decreed. One of the trials of this world is to realize that although one must toil, ultimately his sustenance comes from Hashem.

3) One should not fall into the trap that many fall into; namely to believe that ones livelihood will be affected by other people, and that they have the power to increase or detract from his wealth. The only source of ones wealth is Hashem.

4) It is of great importance to pray every day for ones livelihood, thereby affirming in ones heart these above mentioned ideas. His prayer will help greatly. He should think that his prayers are the primary source of his sustenance and his work secondary. This is expressed in the verse "*And those that seek Hashem will not lack all good.*"

5) The loving kindness of Hashem knows no bounds. If one at times feels that the difficulties of acquiring his livelihood is insurmountable, he should remember that just as the loving kindness of Hashem can produce a mighty tree from a small seed, so too his needs will be met.

תהלים – כג

This Psalm refers to Hashem as a loving shepherd who cares for his flock. Each persons needs are provided for and he feels secure in his closeness to Hashem.

א. מִזְמוֹר לְדָוִד, יְהֹוָה רֹעִי לֹא אֶחְסָר: ב. בִּנְאוֹת דֶּשֶׁא יַרְבִּיצֵנִי, עַל־מֵי מְנֻחוֹת יְנַהֲלֵנִי: ג. נַפְשִׁי יְשׁוֹבֵב, יַנְחֵנִי בְמַעְגְּלֵי־צֶדֶק לְמַעַן שְׁמוֹ: ד. גַּם כִּי־אֵלֵךְ בְּגֵיא צַלְמָוֶת, לֹא־אִירָא רָע כִּי־אַתָּה עִמָּדִי, שִׁבְטְךָ וּמִשְׁעַנְתֶּךָ הֵמָּה יְנַחֲמֻנִי: ה. תַּעֲרֹךְ לְפָנַי שֻׁלְחָן נֶגֶד צֹרְרָי, דִּשַּׁנְתָּ בַשֶּׁמֶן רֹאשִׁי, כּוֹסִי רְוָיָה: ו. אַךְ טוֹב וָחֶסֶד יִרְדְּפוּנִי כָּל־יְמֵי חַיָּי, וְשַׁבְתִּי בְּבֵית־יְהֹוָה לְאֹרֶךְ יָמִים:

תהלים – לד

David composed this Psalm when he was fleeing for his life. Even at this time he was cognizant of all the good that Hashem does and that Hashem provides for all those that trust in him

א. לְדָוִד, בְּשַׁנּוֹתוֹ אֶת־טַעְמוֹ לִפְנֵי אֲבִימֶלֶךְ, וַיְגָרֲשֵׁהוּ וַיֵּלַךְ: ב. אֲבָרֲכָה אֶת־יְהוה בְּכָל־עֵת, תָּמִיד תְּהִלָּתוֹ בְּפִי: ג. בַּיהֹוָה תִּתְהַלֵּל נַפְשִׁי, יִשְׁמְעוּ עֲנָוִים וְיִשְׂמָחוּ: ד. גַּדְּלוּ לַיהֹוָה אִתִּי,

---

1. *In the book of Samuel it relates that when David fled to Avimelech he feigned retardation in order to save himself.*

Psalm – 23

This Psalm refers to Hashem as a loving shepherd who cares for his flock. Each persons needs are provided for and he feels secure in his closeness to Hashem.

1. A Psalm of David; Hashem is my shepherd; I shall not want:

2. He makes me lie down in green pastures; He leads me beside still waters:

3. He restores my soul; He leads me in the paths of righteousness for His name's sake:

4. Even though I walk through the valley of the shadow of death, I will fear no evil; for You are with me; Your rod and Your staff comfort me:

5. You prepare a table before me in the presence of my enemies; You anoint my head with oil; my cup runs over:

6. Surely goodness and loving kindness shall follow me all the days of my life; and I will dwell in the House of Hashem forever:

Psalm – 34

David composed this Psalm when he was fleeing for his life. Even at this time he was cognizant of all the good that Hashem does and that Hashem provides for all those that trust in him

1. A Psalm of David, when he changed his behavior[1] before Avimelech; who drove him away, and he departed:

2. I will bless Hashem at all times; His praise shall continually be in my mouth:

3. My soul shall make her boast in Hashem; the humble shall hear of it, and be glad:

4. O magnify Hashem with me, and let us exalt His name together:

וּנְרוֹמְמָה שְׁמוֹ יַחְדָּו: ה. דָּרַשְׁתִּי אֶת־יהוה
וְעָנָנִי, וּמִכָּל מְגוּרוֹתַי הִצִּילָנִי: ו. הִבִּיטוּ אֵלָיו
וְנָהָרוּ, וּפְנֵיהֶם אַל־יֶחְפָּרוּ: ז. זֶה עָנִי קָרָא,
וַיהוה שָׁמֵעַ, וּמִכָּל־צָרוֹתָיו הוֹשִׁיעוֹ: ח. חֹנֶה
מַלְאַךְ יהוה סָבִיב לִירֵאָיו, וַיְחַלְּצֵם: ט. טַעֲמוּ
וּרְאוּ כִּי טוֹב יהוה, אַשְׁרֵי הַגֶּבֶר יֶחֱסֶה־בּוֹ:
י. יְראוּ אֶת יהוה קְדֹשָׁיו, כִּי־אֵין מַחְסוֹר
לִירֵאָיו: יא. כְּפִירִים רָשׁוּ וְרָעֵבוּ, וְדֹרְשֵׁי יהוה
לֹא יַחְסְרוּ כָל־טוֹב: יב. לְכוּ־בָנִים שִׁמְעוּ־לִי,
יִרְאַת יהוה אֲלַמֶּדְכֶם: יג. מִי־הָאִישׁ הֶחָפֵץ
חַיִּים, אֹהֵב יָמִים לִרְאוֹת טוֹב: יד. נְצֹר לְשׁוֹנְךָ
מֵרָע, וּשְׂפָתֶיךָ מִדַּבֵּר מִרְמָה: טו. סוּר מֵרָע
וַעֲשֵׂה־טוֹב, בַּקֵּשׁ שָׁלוֹם וְרָדְפֵהוּ: טז. עֵינֵי יהוה
אֶל צַדִּיקִים, וְאָזְנָיו אֶל־שַׁוְעָתָם: יז. פְּנֵי יהוה
בְּעֹשֵׂי רָע, לְהַכְרִית מֵאֶרֶץ זִכְרָם: יח. צָעֲקוּ,
וַיהוה שָׁמֵעַ, וּמִכָּל־צָרוֹתָם הִצִּילָם: יט. קָרוֹב
יהוה לְנִשְׁבְּרֵי־לֵב, וְאֶת־דַּכְּאֵי־רוּחַ יוֹשִׁיעַ:
כ. רַבּוֹת רָעוֹת צַדִּיק, וּמִכֻּלָּם יַצִּילֶנּוּ יהוה:
כא. שֹׁמֵר כָּל־עַצְמוֹתָיו, אַחַת מֵהֵנָּה לֹא

5. I sought Hashem, and He answered me, and He saved me from all my fears:

6. They looked to Him, and were radiant; and their faces shall not be ashamed:

7. This poor man cried, and Hashem heard him, and saved him out of all his troubles:

8. The angel of Hashem encamps around those who fear Him, and saves them:

9. O taste and see that Hashem is good; happy is the man who trusts in Him:

10. O fear Hashem, you his pious ones; for those who fear Him have no want:

11. The young lions suffer want and hunger; but those who seek Hashem shall not lack any good:

12. Come, you children, listen to me; I will teach you the fear of Hashem:

13. Who is the man who desires life, and loves many days, that he may see good:[2]

14. Guard your tongue from evil, and your lips from speaking guile:

15. Depart from evil, and do good; seek peace, and pursue it:

16. The eyes of Hashem are upon the righteous, and His ears are open to their cry:

17. The face of Hashem is against those who do evil, to cut off their remembrance from the earth:

18. The [righteous] cry, and Hashem hears, and saves them out of all their troubles:

19. Hashem is near to the broken hearted, and He saves those of a contrite spirit:

20. Many are the afflictions of the righteous; but Hashem saves him from them all:

---

2. *The following verses give the prescription for longevity.*

נִשְׁבָּרָה: כב. תְּמוֹתֵת רָשָׁע רָעָה, וְשֹׂנְאֵי צַדִּיק
יֶאְשָׁמוּ: כג. **פּוֹדֶה** יהוה נֶפֶשׁ עֲבָדָיו, וְלֹא
יֶאְשְׁמוּ כָּל־הַחֹסִים בּוֹ:

תהלים – לו

*The sinner tries to deny the existence of Hashem. But the righteous
realize that all those who seek refuge with Hashem will be protected
and sated from his goodness.*

א. לַמְנַצֵּחַ לְעֶבֶד־יהוה לְדָוִד: ב. נְאֻם־פֶּשַׁע
לָרָשָׁע בְּקֶרֶב לִבִּי, אֵין־פַּחַד אֱלֹהִים לְנֶגֶד
עֵינָיו: ג. כִּי־הֶחֱלִיק אֵלָיו בְּעֵינָיו, לִמְצֹא עֲוֹנוֹ
לִשְׂנֹא: ד. דִּבְרֵי־פִיו אָוֶן וּמִרְמָה, חָדַל לְהַשְׂכִּיל
לְהֵיטִיב: ה. אָוֶן יַחְשֹׁב עַל־מִשְׁכָּבוֹ, יִתְיַצֵּב עַל־
דֶּרֶךְ לֹא־טוֹב, רָע לֹא יִמְאָס: ו. יהוה בְּהַשָּׁמַיִם
חַסְדֶּךָ, אֱמוּנָתְךָ עַד־שְׁחָקִים: ז. צִדְקָתְךָ
כְּהַרְרֵי־אֵל, מִשְׁפָּטֶךָ תְּהוֹם רַבָּה, אָדָם־
וּבְהֵמָה תוֹשִׁיעַ יהוה: ח. מַה־יָּקָר חַסְדְּךָ
אֱלֹהִים, וּבְנֵי אָדָם בְּצֵל כְּנָפֶיךָ יֶחֱסָיוּן: ט. יִרְוְיֻן
מִדֶּשֶׁן בֵּיתֶךָ, וְנַחַל עֲדָנֶיךָ תַשְׁקֵם: י. כִּי־עִמְּךָ
מְקוֹר חַיִּים, בְּאוֹרְךָ נִרְאֶה־אוֹר: יא. מְשֹׁךְ

21.   He guards all his bones; not one of them is broken:

22.   Evil shall slay the wicked; and those who hate the righteous shall be condemned:

23.   Hashem redeems the soul of His servants; and none of those who trust in Him shall be condemned:

Psalm – 36

The sinner tries to deny the existence of Hashem. But the righteous realize that all those who seek refuge with Hashem will be protected and sated from his goodness.

1.   To the chief Musician, A Psalm of David the servant of Hashem:

2.   Transgression speaks to the wicked in his heart, there is no fear of God before his eyes:

3.   For he flatters himself in his own eyes, that his iniquity cannot be found and hated:

4.   The words of his mouth are iniquity and deceit; he has ceased to act wisely, and to do good:

5.   He plots mischief while on his bed; he sets himself in a way that is not good; he does not loathe evil:

6.   Your loving kindness, O Hashem, is in the heavens; and Your faithfulness reaches to the clouds:

7.   Your righteousness is like the great mountains; Your judgments are a great deep; Hashem, You preserve man and beast:

8.   How excellent is Your loving kindness, O God! Therefore the children of men take refuge under the shadow of Your wings:

9.   They shall be abundantly satisfied with the fatness of Your house; and You shall make them drink of the river of Your pleasures:

10.   For with You is the fountain of life; in Your light shall we see light:

11.   O continue Your loving kindness to those who know

חַסְדְּךָ לְיֹדְעֶיךָ, וְצִדְקָתְךָ לְיִשְׁרֵי־לֵב: יב. אַל־
תְּבוֹאֵנִי רֶגֶל גַּאֲוָה, וְיַד־רְשָׁעִים אַל־תְּנִדֵנִי:
יג. שָׁם נָפְלוּ פֹּעֲלֵי אָוֶן, דֹּחוּ, וְלֹא־יָכְלוּ קוּם:

תהלים – סב

In this Psalm, David urges one not to look at the wicked who seem to
succeed through ill gotten means. Rather one should trust in Hashem
for through Him will come the ultimate salvation.

א. לַמְנַצֵּחַ עַל־יְדוּתוּן, מִזְמוֹר לְדָוִד: ב. אַךְ אֶל
אֱלֹהִים דּוּמִיָּה נַפְשִׁי, מִמֶּנּוּ יְשׁוּעָתִי: ג. אַךְ־
הוּא צוּרִי וִישׁוּעָתִי, מִשְׂגַּבִּי, לֹא־אֶמּוֹט רַבָּה:
ד. עַד־אָנָה תְּהוֹתְתוּ עַל־אִישׁ, תְּרָצְּחוּ כֻלְּכֶם
כְּקִיר נָטוּי, גָּדֵר הַדְּחוּיָה: ה. אַךְ מִשְּׂאֵתוֹ יָעֲצוּ
לְהַדִּיחַ, יִרְצוּ כָזָב, בְּפִיו יְבָרֵכוּ, וּבְקִרְבָּם
יְקַלְלוּ־סֶלָה: ו. אַךְ לֵאלֹהִים דּוֹמִּי נַפְשִׁי, כִּי־
מִמֶּנּוּ תִּקְוָתִי: ז. אַךְ־הוּא צוּרִי וִישׁוּעָתִי,
מִשְׂגַּבִּי, לֹא אֶמּוֹט: ח. עַל־אֱלֹהִים יִשְׁעִי
וּכְבוֹדִי, צוּר־עֻזִּי מַחְסִי בֵּאלֹהִים: ט. בִּטְחוּ בוֹ
בְכָל־עֵת, עָם שִׁפְכוּ־לְפָנָיו לְבַבְכֶם, אֱלֹהִים
מַחֲסֶה־לָּנוּ סֶלָה: י. אַךְ הֶבֶל בְּנֵי־אָדָם, כָּזָב בְּנֵי
אִישׁ, בְּמֹאזְנַיִם לַעֲלוֹת הֵמָּה מֵהֶבֶל יָחַד:

You; and Your righteousness to the upright in heart:

12. Let not the foot of arrogance come against me, and let not the hand of the wicked drive me away:

13. There the evildoers have fallen; they are cast down, and are not able to rise:

Psalm – 62

In this Psalm, David urges one not to look at the wicked who seem to succeed through ill gotten means. Rather one should trust in Hashem for through Him will come the ultimate salvation.

1. To the chief Musician, to Jeduthun, A Psalm of David:

2. My soul waits in silence only for God; from Him comes my salvation:

3. He alone is my Rock and my salvation; He is my fortress; I shall not be greatly moved:

4. How long will you seek to overwhelm a man[1]? You will be, all of you, demolished like a leaning wall, or a tottering fence:

5. They even plot to cast him down from his majesty; they delight in lies; they bless with their mouth, but they curse inwardly; Selah:

6. My soul waits only for God in silence; for my hope is from Him:

7. He alone is my Rock and my salvation; He is my refuge; I shall not be moved:

8. In God is my salvation and my glory; the Rock of my strength and my refuge is in God:

9. Trust in Him at all times; you people, pour out your heart before Him; God is a refuge for us; Selah:

10. Surely men of low estate are but a breath, and men of high estate are a lie; to be laid in the scales, they are

---

1. *At this point the Psalmist directs his words to the wicked.*

יא. אַל־ תִּבְטְחוּ בְעֹשֶׁק, וּבְגָזֵל אַל־תֶּהְבָּלוּ, חַיִל כִּי־יָנוּב אַל־תָּשִׁיתוּ לֵב: יב. אַחַת דִּבֶּר אֱלֹהִים, שְׁתַּיִם־זוּ שָׁמָעְתִּי, כִּי עֹז לֵאלֹהִים: יג. וּלְךָ אֲדֹנָי חָסֶד, כִּי־אַתָּה תְשַׁלֵּם לְאִישׁ כְּמַעֲשֵׂהוּ:

תהלים – סה

Hashem controls all forces of nature. When we repent we will become worthy of Divine favor and thus merit the blessings of this world.

א. לַמְנַצֵּחַ מִזְמוֹר לְדָוִד, שִׁיר: ב. לְךָ דֻמִיָּה תְהִלָּה, אֱלֹהִים בְּצִיּוֹן, וּלְךָ יְשֻׁלַּם־נֶדֶר: ג. שֹׁמֵעַ תְּפִלָּה עָדֶיךָ, כָּל־בָּשָׂר יָבֹאוּ: ד. דִּבְרֵי עֲוֹנֹת גָּבְרוּ מֶנִּי, פְּשָׁעֵינוּ אַתָּה תְכַפְּרֵם: ה. אַשְׁרֵי תִּבְחַר וּתְקָרֵב יִשְׁכֹּן חֲצֵרֶיךָ, נִשְׂבְּעָה בְּטוּב בֵּיתֶךָ, קְדֹשׁ הֵיכָלֶךָ: ו. נוֹרָאוֹת בְּצֶדֶק תַּעֲנֵנוּ, אֱלֹהֵי יִשְׁעֵנוּ, מִבְטָח כָּל־קַצְוֵי־אֶרֶץ וְיָם רְחֹקִים: ז. מֵכִין הָרִים בְּכֹחוֹ, נֶאְזָר בִּגְבוּרָה: ח. מַשְׁבִּיחַ שְׁאוֹן יַמִּים, שְׁאוֹן גַּלֵּיהֶם וַהֲמוֹן לְאֻמִּים: ט. וַיִּירְאוּ יֹשְׁבֵי קְצָוֺת מֵאוֹתֹתֶיךָ, מוֹצָאֵי־בֹקֶר וָעֶרֶב תַּרְנִין: י. פָּקַדְתָּ הָאָרֶץ

---

3. *In one of the Commandments of Hashem I heard two things.Firstly, that He will punish the wicked and secondly that the righteous will be rewarded.*

altogether lighter than a breath:[2]

11. Do not trust in oppression, and become not vain in robbery; if riches increase, do not set your heart upon them:

12. God has spoken once; twice have I heard[3] this; that power belongs to God:

13. And to You, O Lord, belongs loving kindness; for You render to every man according to his work:

Psalm – 65

Hashem controls all forces of nature. When we repent we will become worthy of Divine favor and thus merit the blessings of this world.

1. To the chief Musician, A Psalm and Song of David:

2. To You silence is praise, O God, in Zion; and to You shall the vow be fulfilled:

3. O You who hear prayer, to You shall all flesh come:

4. Iniquities prevail against me; as for our transgressions, You shall purge them away:

5. Happy is the man whom You choose, and bring near, that he may dwell in Your courts; we shall be satisfied with the goodness of Your house, of Your Holy Temple:

6. By awesome things in righteousness will You answer us, O God of our salvation; You are the confidence of all the ends of the earth, and of the farthest sea:

7. Who by His strength has established the mountains; being girded with power:

8. Who stills the noise of the seas, the roaring of their waves, and the tumult of the peoples:

9. And those who dwell in the outermost parts are afraid of Your signs; You make the outgoings of the morning and evening to rejoice:

10. You visit the earth, and water it; You greatly enrich it

---

2. *When the wicked are placed on the scale they are equal to naught.*

וַתְּשֹׁקְקֶהָ, רַבַּת תַּעְשְׁרֶנָּה פֶּלֶג אֱלֹהִים מָלֵא
מָיִם, תָּכִין דְּגָנָם כִּי־כֵן תְּכִינֶהָ: יא. תְּלָמֶיהָ רַוֵּה
נַחֵת גְּדוּדֶיהָ, בִּרְבִיבִים תְּמֹגְגֶנָּה, צִמְחָהּ
תְּבָרֵךְ: יב. עִטַּרְתָּ שְׁנַת טוֹבָתֶךָ, וּמַעְגָּלֶיךָ
יִרְעֲפוּן דָּשֶׁן: יג. יִרְעֲפוּ נְאוֹת מִדְבָּר, וְגִיל
גְּבָעוֹת תַּחְגֹּרְנָה: יד. לָבְשׁוּ כָרִים הַצֹּאן,
וַעֲמָקִים יַעַטְפוּ־בָר, יִתְרוֹעֲעוּ אַף יָשִׁירוּ:

תהלים – סז

We ask for Divine favor and blessing which will raise this world to
perfection. This will cause the land to give forth its produce and
sustain mankind.

א. לַמְנַצֵּחַ בִּנְגִינֹת, מִזְמוֹר שִׁיר: ב. אֱלֹהִים יְחָנֵּנוּ
וִיבָרְכֵנוּ, יָאֵר פָּנָיו אִתָּנוּ סֶלָה: ג. לָדַעַת בָּאָרֶץ
דַּרְכֶּךָ, בְּכָל־גּוֹיִם יְשׁוּעָתֶךָ: ד. יוֹדוּךָ עַמִּים
אֱלֹהִים, יוֹדוּךָ עַמִּים כֻּלָּם: ה. יִשְׂמְחוּ וִירַנְּנוּ
לְאֻמִּים, כִּי־תִשְׁפֹּט עַמִּים מִישׁוֹר, וּלְאֻמִּים
בָּאָרֶץ תַּנְחֵם סֶלָה: ו. יוֹדוּךָ עַמִּים אֱלֹהִים,
יוֹדוּךָ עַמִּים כֻּלָּם: ז. אֶרֶץ נָתְנָה יְבוּלָהּ, יְבָרְכֵנוּ
אֱלֹהִים אֱלֹהֵינוּ: ח. יְבָרְכֵנוּ אֱלֹהִים, וְיִירְאוּ
אֹתוֹ כָּל־אַפְסֵי־אָרֶץ:

24

with the river of God, which is full of water; You provide their grain, for You have prepared it:

11. You water her furrows abundantly; You settle her ridges; You make it soft with showers; You bless its growth:

12. You crown the year with Your goodness; and Your paths drop fatness:

13. The pastures of the wilderness drip; and the hills rejoice on every side:

14. The meadows are clothed with flocks; the valleys also are covered over with grain; they shout for joy, they also sing:

Psalm – 67

We ask for Divine favor and blessing which will raise this world to perfection. This will cause the land to give forth its produce and sustain mankind.

1. To the chief Musician for stringed instruments, A Psalm Song:

2. God be gracious to us, and bless us; and let His face shine upon us; Selah:

3. That Your way may be known on earth, Your salvation among all nations:

4. Let the peoples praise You, O God; let all the peoples praise You:

5. O let the nations be glad and sing for joy; for You shall judge the peoples righteously, and govern the nations on earth; Selah:

6. Let the peoples praise You, O God; let all the peoples praiseYou:

7. The earth has yielded her produce; and God, our own God, shall bless us:

8. God shall bless us; let all the ends of the earth fear Him:

תהלים – פה

We beg Hashem to accept our repentance and return to us. Unity between us and Hashem will cause the land to give forth its produce.

א. לַמְנַצֵּחַ, לִבְנֵי קֹרַח מִזְמוֹר: ב. רָצִיתָ יְהוָה אַרְצֶךָ, שַׁבְתָּ שְׁבִית יַעֲקֹב: ג. נָשָׂאתָ עֲוֹן עַמֶּךָ, כִּסִּיתָ כָל חַטָּאתָם סֶלָה: ד. אָסַפְתָּ כָל עֶבְרָתֶךָ, הֱשִׁיבוֹתָ מֵחֲרוֹן אַפֶּךָ: ה. שׁוּבֵנוּ אֱלֹהֵי יִשְׁעֵנוּ, וְהָפֵר כַּעַסְךָ עִמָּנוּ: ו. הַלְעוֹלָם תֶּאֱנַף בָּנוּ, תִּמְשֹׁךְ אַפְּךָ לְדֹר וָדֹר: ז. הֲלֹא אַתָּה תָּשׁוּב תְּחַיֵּינוּ, וְעַמְּךָ יִשְׂמְחוּ בָךְ: ח. הַרְאֵנוּ יְהוָה חַסְדֶּךָ, וְיֶשְׁעֲךָ תִּתֶּן לָנוּ: ט. אֶשְׁמְעָה מַה יְדַבֵּר הָאֵל יְהוָה, כִּי יְדַבֵּר שָׁלוֹם אֶל עַמּוֹ וְאֶל חֲסִידָיו, וְאַל יָשׁוּבוּ לְכִסְלָה: י. אַךְ קָרוֹב לִירֵאָיו יִשְׁעוֹ, לִשְׁכֹּן כָּבוֹד בְּאַרְצֵנוּ: יא. חֶסֶד וֶאֱמֶת נִפְגָּשׁוּ, צֶדֶק וְשָׁלוֹם נָשָׁקוּ: יב. אֱמֶת מֵאֶרֶץ תִּצְמָח, וְצֶדֶק מִשָּׁמַיִם נִשְׁקָף: יג. גַּם יְהוָה יִתֵּן הַטּוֹב, וְאַרְצֵנוּ תִּתֵּן יְבוּלָהּ: יד. צֶדֶק לְפָנָיו יְהַלֵּךְ, וְיָשֵׂם לְדֶרֶךְ פְּעָמָיו:

Psalm – 85

We beg Hashem to accept our repentance and return to us. Unity between us and Hashem will cause the land to give forth its produce.

1. To the chief Musician, A Psalm for the sons of Korah:

2. Hashem, You have been favorable to Your land; You have brought back the captivity of Jacob:

3. You have forgiven the iniquity of Your people, You have pardoned all their sin; Selah:

4. You have withdrawn all Your wrath; You have turned from the fierceness of Your anger:

5. Restore us, O God of our salvation, and cease Your anger toward us:

6. Will You be angry with us for ever? Will You draw out Your anger to all generations:

7. Will You not revive us again, that Your people may rejoice in You:

8. Show us Your loving kindness, O Hashem, and grant us Your salvation:

9. I will hear what God, Hashem, will speak; for He will speak peace to His people, and to His pious ones; but let them not turn back to folly:

10. Surely His salvation is near to those who fear Him; that glory may dwell in our land:

11. Loving kindness and truth meet together; righteousness and peace kiss each other:

12. Truth shall spring from the earth; and righteousness shall look down from heaven:

13. Also, Hashem shall give that which is good; and our land shall yield her produce:

14. Righteousness shall go before Him; and walk in the way of His steps:

תהלים - קד

This Psalm praises Hashem for the beautiful world that He created. He provides sustenance for all its inhabitants.

א. בָּרְכִי נַפְשִׁי אֶת־יְהֹוָה, יְהֹוָה אֱלֹהַי גָּדַלְתָּ מְּאֹד, הוֹד וְהָדָר לָבָשְׁתָּ: ב. עֹטֶה־אוֹר כַּשַּׂלְמָה, נוֹטֶה שָׁמַיִם כַּיְרִיעָה: ג. הַמְקָרֶה בַמַּיִם עֲלִיּוֹתָיו, הַשָּׂם־עָבִים רְכוּבוֹ, הַמְהַלֵּךְ עַל־כַּנְפֵי רוּחַ: ד. עֹשֶׂה מַלְאָכָיו רוּחוֹת, מְשָׁרְתָיו אֵשׁ לֹהֵט: ה. יָסַד־אֶרֶץ עַל־מְכוֹנֶיהָ, בַּל־תִּמּוֹט עוֹלָם וָעֶד: ו. תְּהוֹם כַּלְּבוּשׁ כִּסִּיתוֹ, עַל־הָרִים יַעַמְדוּ מָיִם: ז. מִן־גַּעֲרָתְךָ יְנוּסוּן, מִן־קוֹל רַעַמְךָ יֵחָפֵזוּן: ח. יַעֲלוּ הָרִים יֵרְדוּ בְקָעוֹת, אֶל־מְקוֹם זֶה יָסַדְתָּ לָהֶם: ט. גְּבוּל־שַׂמְתָּ בַּל־יַעֲבֹרוּן, בַּל־יְשֻׁבוּן לְכַסּוֹת הָאָרֶץ: י. הַמְשַׁלֵּחַ מַעְיָנִים בַּנְּחָלִים, בֵּין הָרִים יְהַלֵּכוּן: יא. יַשְׁקוּ כָּל־חַיְתוֹ שָׂדָי, יִשְׁבְּרוּ פְרָאִים צְמָאָם: יב. עֲלֵיהֶם עוֹף־הַשָּׁמַיִם יִשְׁכּוֹן, מִבֵּין עֳפָאיִם יִתְּנוּ־קוֹל: יג. מַשְׁקֶה הָרִים מֵעֲלִיּוֹתָיו, מִפְּרִי מַעֲשֶׂיךָ תִּשְׂבַּע הָאָרֶץ: יד. מַצְמִיחַ חָצִיר

---

2. *During the time of creation the waters heard the thunderous call of Hashem to gather together and let the land be revealed.*

Psalm – 104

This Psalm praises Hashem for the beautiful world that He created. He provides sustenance for all its inhabitants.

1. Bless Hashem, O my soul; Hashem my God, You are very great; You are clothed with glory and majesty:

2. Who covers Himself with light as with a garment; Who stretches out the heavens like a curtain:

3. Who lays the rafters of His chambers with waters; Who makes the clouds His chariot; Who walks upon the wings of the wind:

4. Who makes the winds His messengers; the flames of fire His ministers:

5. Who laid the foundations of the earth, that it should not move forever:

6. You covered it with the deep[1] as with a garment; the waters stood upon the mountains:

7. At Your rebuke they fled[2]; at the voice of Your thunder they hurried away:

8. They went up the mountains; they flowed down the valleys to the place which You appointed for them:

9. You have set a bound that they may not pass, so that they might not again cover the earth:

10. He sends the springs into the valleys, they flow between the mountains:

11. They give drink to every beast of the field; the wild asses quench their thirst:

12. Beside them dwell the birds of the sky, among the branches they sing:

13. He waters the mountains from His high abode; the earth is satisfied with the fruit of Your works:

14. He makes the grass grow for the cattle, and plants for the service of man, that He may bring forth food from the earth:

---

1. *The deep refers to the oceans that cover the earth.*

לַבְּהֵמָה, וְעֵשֶׂב לַעֲבֹדַת הָאָדָם, לְהוֹצִיא
לֶחֶם מִן־הָאָרֶץ: טו. וְיַיִן יְשַׂמַּח לְבַב־אֱנוֹשׁ,
לְהַצְהִיל פָּנִים מִשָּׁמֶן, וְלֶחֶם לְבַב־אֱנוֹשׁ יִסְעָד:
טז. יִשְׂבְּעוּ עֲצֵי יְהוָה, אַרְזֵי לְבָנוֹן אֲשֶׁר נָטָע:
יז. אֲשֶׁר־שָׁם צִפֳּרִים יְקַנֵּנוּ, חֲסִידָה בְּרוֹשִׁים
בֵּיתָהּ: יח. הָרִים הַגְּבֹהִים לַיְּעֵלִים, סְלָעִים
מַחְסֶה לַשְׁפַנִּים: יט. עָשָׂה יָרֵחַ לְמוֹעֲדִים, שֶׁמֶשׁ
יָדַע מְבוֹאוֹ: כ. תָּשֶׁת־חֹשֶׁךְ וִיהִי לָיְלָה, בּוֹ־
תִרְמֹשׂ כָּל־חַיְתוֹ־יָעַר: כא. הַכְּפִירִים שֹׁאֲגִים
לַטָּרֶף, וּלְבַקֵּשׁ מֵאֵל אָכְלָם: כב. תִּזְרַח הַשֶּׁמֶשׁ
יֵאָסֵפוּן, וְאֶל־מְעוֹנֹתָם יִרְבָּצוּן: כג. יֵצֵא אָדָם
לְפָעֳלוֹ, וְלַעֲבֹדָתוֹ עֲדֵי־עָרֶב: כד. מָה־רַבּוּ
מַעֲשֶׂיךָ יְהוָה, כֻּלָּם בְּחָכְמָה עָשִׂיתָ, מָלְאָה
הָאָרֶץ קִנְיָנֶךָ: כה. זֶה הַיָּם גָּדוֹל וּרְחַב יָדָיִם,
שָׁם־רֶמֶשׂ וְאֵין מִסְפָּר, חַיּוֹת קְטַנּוֹת עִם־
גְּדֹלוֹת: כו. שָׁם אֳנִיּוֹת יְהַלֵּכוּן, לִוְיָתָן זֶה־יָצַרְתָּ
לְשַׂחֶק־בּוֹ: כז. כֻּלָּם אֵלֶיךָ יְשַׂבֵּרוּן, לָתֵת אָכְלָם
בְּעִתּוֹ: כח. תִּתֵּן לָהֶם יִלְקֹטוּן, תִּפְתַּח יָדְךָ
יִשְׂבְּעוּן טוֹב: כט. תַּסְתִּיר פָּנֶיךָ יִבָּהֵלוּן, תֹּסֵף
רוּחָם יִגְוָעוּן, וְאֶל־עֲפָרָם יְשׁוּבוּן: ל. תְּשַׁלַּח

15. And wine that gladdens the heart of man, and oil to make his face shine, and bread which strengthens man's heart:

16. The trees of Hashem have their fill; the cedars of Lebanon, which He has planted:

17. Where the birds make their nests; as for the stork, the cypress trees are her house:

18. The high mountains are a refuge for the wild goats; and the rocks for the badgers:

19. He appointed the moon for seasons; the sun knows its setting time:

20. You make darkness, and it is night; when all the beasts of the forest creep forth:

21. The young lions roar for their prey, and seek their food from God:

22. The sun rises, they gather themselves together, and lie down in their dens:

23. Man goes forth to his work and to his labor until the evening:

24. Hashem, how manifold are your works! In wisdom you have made them all; the earth is full of your creatures:

25. So is this great and wide sea, where there are innumerable creeping things, living things, both small and great:

26. There go the ships; and Leviathan which you have made to play in it:

27. These wait all upon You; that You may give them their food in due time:

28. When You give to them they gather it up; when You open Your hand, they are filled with good:

29. When You hide Your face, they are troubled; when You take away their breath, they die, and return to their dust:

30. When You send forth Your breath, they are created; and You renew the face of the earth:

רוּחֲךָ יִבָּרֵאוּן, וּתְחַדֵּשׁ פְּנֵי אֲדָמָה: לא. יְהִי
כְבוֹד יְהֹוָה לְעוֹלָם, יִשְׂמַח יְהֹוָה בְּמַעֲשָׂיו:
לב. הַמַּבִּיט לָאָרֶץ וַתִּרְעָד, יִגַּע בֶּהָרִים וְיֶעֱשָׁנוּ:
לג. אָשִׁירָה לַיהֹוָה בְּחַיָּי, אֲזַמְּרָה לֵאלֹהַי
בְּעוֹדִי: לד. יֶעֱרַב עָלָיו שִׂיחִי, אָנֹכִי אֶשְׂמַח
בַּיהֹוָה: לה. יִתַּמּוּ חַטָּאִים מִן־הָאָרֶץ, וּרְשָׁעִים
עוֹד אֵינָם, בָּרְכִי נַפְשִׁי אֶת־יְהֹוָה הַלְלוּיָהּ:

תהלים – קכא

This Psalm describes one who lifts his eyes to Hashem and comes to realize that all his needs come only from Hashem.

א. שִׁיר לַמַּעֲלוֹת, אֶשָּׂא עֵינַי אֶל־הֶהָרִים, מֵאַיִן
יָבוֹא עֶזְרִי: ב. עֶזְרִי מֵעִם יְהֹוָה, עֹשֵׂה שָׁמַיִם
וָאָרֶץ: ג. אַל־יִתֵּן לַמּוֹט רַגְלֶךָ, אַל־יָנוּם שֹׁמְרֶךָ:
ד. הִנֵּה לֹא־יָנוּם וְלֹא יִישָׁן, שׁוֹמֵר יִשְׂרָאֵל:
ה. יְהֹוָה שֹׁמְרֶךָ, יְהֹוָה צִלְּךָ עַל־יַד יְמִינֶךָ:
ו. יוֹמָם הַשֶּׁמֶשׁ לֹא־יַכֶּכָּה, וְיָרֵחַ בַּלָּיְלָה: ז. יְהֹוָה
יִשְׁמָרְךָ מִכָּל־רָע, יִשְׁמֹר אֶת־נַפְשֶׁךָ: ח. יְהֹוָה
יִשְׁמָר צֵאתְךָ וּבוֹאֶךָ, מֵעַתָּה וְעַד־עוֹלָם:

---

ascending to the sanctuary in the Bais Hamikdosh.
2. Hashem will protect you as one shaded from the sun.

31. May the glory of Hashem endure forever; may Hashem rejoice in his works:

32. He looks on the earth, and it trembles; He touches the mountains, and they smoke:

33. I will sing to Hashem as long as I live; I will sing praise to my God while I have my being:

34. My praises of Him shall be sweet; I will rejoice in Hashem:

35. Let the sinners be consumed from the earth, and let the wicked be no more; Bless Hashem, O my soul; Halleluyah:

Psalm – 121

This Psalm describes one who lifts his eyes to Hashem and comes to realize that all his needs come only from Hashem.

1. A Song of ascents[1]; I will lift up my eyes to the mountains. From where does my help come?

2. My help comes from Hashem, Who made heaven and earth.

3. He will not let your foot falter; your guardian will not slumber:

4. Behold, He who guards Israel shall neither slumber nor sleep:

5. Hashem is your keeper; Hashem is your shade[2] upon your right hand:

6. The sun shall not strike you by day, nor the moon by night:

7. Hashem shall preserve you from all evil; He shall preserve your soul:

8. Hashem shall preserve your going out and your coming in from this time forth, and forever:

---

1. *This Psalm was written to be sung by the Levites while standing on the steps*

תהלים - קלו

All twenty six verses of this Psalm end with the phrase "for His loving kindness endures forever". It delineates all the good that Hashem has done for us over the generations.

א. הוֹדוּ לַיהוָה כִּי־טוֹב, כִּי לְעוֹלָם חַסְדּוֹ:

ב. הוֹדוּ לֵאלֹהֵי הָאֱלֹהִים, כִּי לְעוֹלָם חַסְדּוֹ:

ג. הוֹדוּ לַאֲדֹנֵי הָאֲדֹנִים, כִּי לְעוֹלָם חַסְדּוֹ:

ד. לְעֹשֵׂה נִפְלָאוֹת גְּדֹלוֹת לְבַדּוֹ, כִּי לְעוֹלָם חַסְדּוֹ: ה. לְעֹשֵׂה הַשָּׁמַיִם בִּתְבוּנָה, כִּי לְעוֹלָם חַסְדּוֹ: ו. לְרֹקַע הָאָרֶץ עַל־הַמָּיִם, כִּי לְעוֹלָם חַסְדּוֹ: ז. לְעֹשֵׂה אוֹרִים גְּדֹלִים, כִּי לְעוֹלָם חַסְדּוֹ: ח. אֶת־הַשֶּׁמֶשׁ לְמֶמְשֶׁלֶת בַּיּוֹם, כִּי לְעוֹלָם חַסְדּוֹ: ט. אֶת־הַיָּרֵחַ וְכוֹכָבִים לְמֶמְשְׁלוֹת בַּלָּיְלָה, כִּי לְעוֹלָם חַסְדּוֹ: י. לְמַכֵּה מִצְרַיִם בִּבְכוֹרֵיהֶם, כִּי לְעוֹלָם חַסְדּוֹ: יא. וַיּוֹצֵא יִשְׂרָאֵל מִתּוֹכָם, כִּי לְעוֹלָם חַסְדּוֹ: יב. בְּיָד חֲזָקָה וּבִזְרוֹעַ נְטוּיָה, כִּי לְעוֹלָם חַסְדּוֹ: יג. לְגֹזֵר יַם־סוּף לִגְזָרִים, כִּי לְעוֹלָם חַסְדּוֹ: יד. וְהֶעֱבִיר

2. When the earth and heavens were created there were no angels yet.

3. Our sages teach us that before the plague of the first born the first born rebelled and fought against the Egyptians.

4. Our sages teach, that the red sea was parted into many parts.

Psalm – 136

All twenty six verses of this Psalm end with the phrase "for His loving kindness endures forever". It delineates all the good that Hashem has done for us over the generations.

1. O give thanks to Hashem; for He is good; for His loving kindness endures for ever[1]:

2. O give thanks to the God of gods; for His loving kindness endures for ever:

3. O give thanks to the Lord of lords; for His loving kindness endures for ever:

4. To Him who alone[2] does great wonders; for His loving kindness endures for ever:

5. To He who with understanding made the heavens; for His loving kindness endures for ever:

6. To Him who stretched out the earth above the waters; for His loving kindness endures for ever:

7. To Him who made the great lights; for His loving kindness endures for ever:

8. The sun to rule by day; for His loving kindness endures for ever:

9. The moon and the stars to rule by night; for His loving kindness endures for ever:

10. To Him who struck Egypt with their firstborn[3]; for His loving kindness endures for ever:

11. And He brought out Israel from among them; for His loving kindness endures for ever:

12. With a strong hand, and with a stretched out arm; for His loving kindness endures for ever:

13. To Him who parted the Red Sea into paths[4]; for His loving kindness endures for ever:

14. And He passed Israel through the midst of it; for His loving kindness endures for ever:

---

1. *For His kindness endures forever, unlike the kindness of man.*

יִשְׂרָאֵל בְּתוֹכוֹ, כִּי לְעוֹלָם חַסְדּוֹ: טו. וְנִעֵר

פַּרְעֹה וְחֵילוֹ בְיַם־סוּף, כִּי לְעוֹלָם חַסְדּוֹ:

טז. לְמוֹלִיךְ עַמּוֹ בַּמִּדְבָּר, כִּי לְעוֹלָם חַסְדּוֹ:

יז. לְמַכֵּה מְלָכִים גְּדֹלִים, כִּי לְעוֹלָם חַסְדּוֹ:

יח. וַיַּהֲרֹג מְלָכִים אַדִּירִים, כִּי לְעוֹלָם חַסְדּוֹ:

יט. לְסִיחוֹן מֶלֶךְ הָאֱמֹרִי, כִּי לְעוֹלָם חַסְדּוֹ:

כ. וּלְעוֹג מֶלֶךְ הַבָּשָׁן, כִּי לְעוֹלָם חַסְדּוֹ: כא. וְנָתַן

אַרְצָם לְנַחֲלָה, כִּי לְעוֹלָם חַסְדּוֹ: כב. נַחֲלָה

לְיִשְׂרָאֵל עַבְדּוֹ, כִּי לְעוֹלָם חַסְדּוֹ:

כג. שֶׁבְּשִׁפְלֵנוּ זָכַר לָנוּ, כִּי לְעוֹלָם חַסְדּוֹ:

כד. וַיִּפְרְקֵנוּ מִצָּרֵינוּ, כִּי לְעוֹלָם חַסְדּוֹ: כה. נֹתֵן

לֶחֶם לְכָל־בָּשָׂר, כִּי לְעוֹלָם חַסְדּוֹ: כו. הוֹדוּ

לְאֵל הַשָּׁמָיִם, כִּי לְעוֹלָם חַסְדּוֹ:

תהלים – קמד

David in this Psalm attributes his success in all of his endeavors to the inspiration and help of Hashem.

א. לְדָוִד, בָּרוּךְ יְהוָה צוּרִי, הַמְלַמֵּד יָדַי לַקְרָב,

---

us is as great an achievement as the splitting of the red sea.

7. *The heaven is the source of rain which causes the bread to grow; so we praise the God of heaven for the sustenance he provides.*

15. And threw Pharaoh and his army in the Red Sea; for His loving kindness endures for ever:

16. To Him who led his people through the wilderness; for His loving kindness endures for ever:

17. To Him who struck great kings; for His loving kindness endures for ever:

18. And slew great kings; for His loving kindness endures for ever:

19. Sihon king of the Amorites; for His loving kindness endures for ever:

20. And Og the king of Bashan; for His loving kindness endures for ever:

21. And gave their land for a heritage; for His loving kindness endures for ever:

22. A heritage to Israel His servant; for His loving kindness endures for ever:

23. Who remembered us in our low estate[5]; for His loving kindness endures for ever:

24. And has redeemed us from our enemies; for His loving kindness endures for ever:

25. Who gives bread to all flesh[6]; for His loving kindness endures for ever:

26. O give thanks to the God of heaven[7]; for His loving kindness endures for ever:

Psalm – 144

David in this Psalm attributes his success in all of his endeavors to the inspiration and help of Hashem.

1. A Psalm of David; Blessed be Hashem my strength, Who teaches my hands to war, and my fingers to fight:

---

5. *Even when we are unable to keep the Torah because of the travails of exile He still helps us on the account of His loving kindness. (Chida)*

6. *After reminiscing all the wonders of creation and the exodus from Egypt the Psalmist mentions the kindness of providing sustenance which our sages teach*

אֶצְבְּעוֹתַי לַמִּלְחָמָה: ב. חַסְדִּי וּמְצוּדָתִי מִשְׂגַּבִּי וּמְפַלְטִי לִי, מָגִנִּי, וּבוֹ חָסִיתִי, הָרוֹדֵד עַמִּי תַחְתָּי: ג. יְהוָה מָה־אָדָם וַתֵּדָעֵהוּ, בֶּן־אֱנוֹשׁ וַתְּחַשְּׁבֵהוּ: ד. אָדָם לַהֶבֶל דָּמָה, יָמָיו כְּצֵל עוֹבֵר: ה. יְהוָה הַט־שָׁמֶיךָ וְתֵרֵד, גַּע בֶּהָרִים וְיֶעֱשָׁנוּ: ו. בְּרוֹק בָּרָק וּתְפִיצֵם, שְׁלַח חִצֶּיךָ וּתְהֻמֵּם: ז. שְׁלַח יָדֶיךָ מִמָּרוֹם, פְּצֵנִי וְהַצִּילֵנִי מִמַּיִם רַבִּים, מִיַּד בְּנֵי נֵכָר: ח. אֲשֶׁר פִּיהֶם דִּבֶּר שָׁוְא, וִימִינָם יְמִין שָׁקֶר: ט. אֱלֹהִים שִׁיר חָדָשׁ אָשִׁירָה לָּךְ, בְּנֵבֶל עָשׂוֹר אֲזַמְּרָה־לָּךְ: י. הַנּוֹתֵן תְּשׁוּעָה לַמְּלָכִים, הַפּוֹצֶה אֶת־דָּוִד עַבְדּוֹ, מֵחֶרֶב רָעָה: יא. פְּצֵנִי וְהַצִּילֵנִי מִיַּד בְּנֵי־נֵכָר, אֲשֶׁר פִּיהֶם דִּבֶּר־שָׁוְא, וִימִינָם יְמִין שָׁקֶר: יב. אֲשֶׁר בָּנֵינוּ כִּנְטִעִים, מְגֻדָּלִים בִּנְעוּרֵיהֶם, בְּנוֹתֵינוּ כְזָוִיֹּת, מְחֻטָּבוֹת תַּבְנִית הֵיכָל: יג. מְזָוֵינוּ מְלֵאִים מְפִיקִים מִזַּן אֶל־זַן, צֹאונֵנוּ מַאֲלִיפוֹת, מְרֻבָּבוֹת בְּחוּצוֹתֵינוּ: יד. אַלּוּפֵינוּ מְסֻבָּלִים, אֵין־פֶּרֶץ וְאֵין יוֹצֵאת, וְאֵין צְוָחָה בִּרְחֹבֹתֵינוּ: טו. אַשְׁרֵי הָעָם שֶׁכָּכָה לּוֹ אַשְׁרֵי הָעָם שֶׁיְּהוָה אֱלֹהָיו:

2. My gracious one, and my fortress; my high tower, and my savior; my shield, and He in whom I trust; Who subdues my people under me:

3. Hashem, what is man, that You should take knowledge of him, or the son of man, that You should take account of him:

4. Man is like a breath; his days are like a passing shadow:

5. Bow Your heavens, Hashem, and come down; touch the mountains, and they shall smoke:

6. Cast forth lightning, and scatter them; shoot out Your arrows, and destroy them:

7. Send Your hand from above; rescue me, and save me from great waters, from the hand of strangers:

8. Whose mouth speak vanity, and their right hand is a right hand of falsehood:

9. I will sing a new song to You, O God; on a harp of ten strings will I sing praises to You:

10. It is He who gives salvation to kings; Who saves David His servant from the harmful sword:

11. Rescue and save me from the hand of strangers, whose mouth speaks vanity, and their right hand is a right hand of falsehood:

12. May our sons be like plants grown up in their youth! May our daughters be like cornerstones, cut for the structure of a palace:

13. May our garners be full, affording all manner of store! May our sheep bring forth thousands and ten thousands in our fields:

14. May our oxen be heavy laden, so there should be no breach or migration! May there be no loud cry in our in our streets:

15. Happy is the people to whom that is the case! Happy is the people whose God is Hashem:

תהלים קמה

This Psalm proclaims the power of Hashem over all creation, and that
all living things are sustained by Him.

א. תְּהִלָּה לְדָוִד, אֲרוֹמִמְךָ אֱלוֹהַי הַמֶּלֶךְ, וַאֲבָרְכָה שִׁמְךָ לְעוֹלָם וָעֶד: ב. בְּכָל־יוֹם אֲבָרְכֶךָּ, וַאֲהַלְלָה שִׁמְךָ לְעוֹלָם וָעֶד: ג. גָּדוֹל יְהוָה וּמְהֻלָּל מְאֹד, וְלִגְדֻלָּתוֹ אֵין חֵקֶר: ד. דּוֹר לְדוֹר יְשַׁבַּח מַעֲשֶׂיךָ, וּגְבוּרֹתֶיךָ יַגִּידוּ: ה. הֲדַר כְּבוֹד הוֹדֶךָ, וְדִבְרֵי נִפְלְאוֹתֶיךָ אָשִׂיחָה: ו. וֶעֱזוּז נוֹרְאֹתֶיךָ יֹאמֵרוּ, וּגְדוּלָּתְךָ אֲסַפְּרֶנָּה: ז. זֵכֶר רַב־טוּבְךָ יַבִּיעוּ, וְצִדְקָתְךָ יְרַנֵּנוּ: ח. חַנּוּן וְרַחוּם יְהוָה, אֶרֶךְ אַפַּיִם וּגְדָל־חָסֶד: ט. טוֹב־יְהוָה לַכֹּל, וְרַחֲמָיו עַל־כָּל־מַעֲשָׂיו: י. יוֹדוּךָ יְהוָה כָּל מַעֲשֶׂיךָ, וַחֲסִידֶיךָ יְבָרְכוּכָה: יא. כְּבוֹד מַלְכוּתְךָ יֹאמֵרוּ, וּגְבוּרָתְךָ יְדַבֵּרוּ: יב. לְהוֹדִיעַ לִבְנֵי הָאָדָם גְּבוּרֹתָיו, וּכְבוֹד הֲדַר מַלְכוּתוֹ: יג. מַלְכוּתְךָ מַלְכוּת כָּל־עֹלָמִים, וּמֶמְשַׁלְתְּךָ בְּכָל־דּוֹר וָדוֹר: יד. סוֹמֵךְ יְהוָה לְכָל־הַנֹּפְלִים, וְזוֹקֵף לְכָל־הַכְּפוּפִים: טו. עֵינֵי־כֹל אֵלֶיךָ יְשַׂבֵּרוּ, וְאַתָּה נוֹתֵן־לָהֶם אֶת־אָכְלָם בְּעִתּוֹ:

40

Psalm – 145

This Psalm proclaims the power of Hashem over all creation, and that all living things are sustained by Him.

1. David's Psalm of praise; I will extol You, my God, O king; and I will bless Your name forever and ever:

2. Every day I will bless You; and I will praise Your Name forever and ever:

3. Great is Hashem, and greatly to be praised; and His greatness is unsearchable:

4. One generation shall praise Your works to the next, and shall declare Your mighty acts:

5. I will speak of the glorious splendor of Your majesty, and of Your wondrous works:

6. And men shall speak of the might of Your awesome acts; and I will declare Your greatness:

7. They shall utter the fame of Your great goodness, and shall sing of Your righteousness:

8. Hashem is gracious, and full of compassion; slow to anger, and of abundant loving kindness:

9. Hashem is good to all; and His mercies are over all His works:

10. All Your works shall praise You, O Hashem; and Your pious ones shall bless You:

11. They shall speak of the glory of Your kingdom, and talk of Your power:

12. To make known to the sons of men His mighty acts, and the glorious majesty of His kingdom:

13. Your kingdom is an everlasting kingdom, and Your dominion endures throughout all generations:

14. Hashem upholds all who fall, and raises up all those who are bowed down:

15. The eyes of all wait upon You; and You give them their food in due season:

טז. **פּוֹתֵחַ** אֶת־יָדֶךָ, וּמַשְׂבִּיעַ לְכָל־חַי רָצוֹן:

יז. **צַדִּיק** יְהוָה בְּכָל־דְּרָכָיו, וְחָסִיד בְּכָל־מַעֲשָׂיו:

יח. **קָרוֹב** יְהוָה לְכָל־קֹרְאָיו, לְכֹל אֲשֶׁר יִקְרָאֻהוּ בֶאֱמֶת: יט. **רְצוֹן־**יְרֵאָיו יַעֲשֶׂה, וְאֶת־שַׁוְעָתָם יִשְׁמַע וְיוֹשִׁיעֵם: כ. **שׁוֹמֵר** יְהוָה אֶת־כָּל־אֹהֲבָיו, וְאֵת כָּל־הָרְשָׁעִים יַשְׁמִיד: כא. **תְּהִלַּת** יְהוָה יְדַבֶּר־פִּי, וִיבָרֵךְ כָּל־בָּשָׂר שֵׁם קָדְשׁוֹ לְעוֹלָם וָעֶד:

16. You open Your hand, and satisfy the desire of every living thing:

17. Hashem is righteous in all His ways, and gracious in all His works:

18. Hashem is near to all those who call upon Him, to all who call upon Him in truth:

19. He will fulfil the desire of those who fear Him; He also will hear their cry, and will save them:

20. Hashem preserves all those who love Him; but all the wicked He will destroy:

21. My mouth shall speak the praise of Hashem; and let all flesh bless His Holy Name forever and ever:

*The early authorities recommended reciting the Section of the Manna
as a merit for a livelihood. (See Mishnah Berurah O.C. 1,5)
Just as the Manna was food provided directly by Hashem, so too must
one realize that although he toils and puts in effort, his livelihood
ultimately comes from Hashem. Indeed, Hashem commanded Moshe to
save a container of Manna for future generations to remind them that
livelihood is in Hashem's hands.*

תפילה על הפרנסה

יְהִי רָצוֹן מִלְּפָנֶיךָ יְהוָֹה אֱלֹהֵינוּ וֵאלֹהֵי אֲבוֹתֵינוּ שֶׁתַּזְמִין
פַּרְנָסָה לְכָל עַמְּךָ בֵּית יִשְׂרָאֵל וּפַרְנָסָתִי וּפַרְנָסַת אַנְשֵׁי
בֵיתִי בִּכְלָלָם. בְּנַחַת וְלֹא בְּצַעַר בְּכָבוֹד וְלֹא בְּבִזּוּי בְּהֶתֵּר
וְלֹא בְּאִסוּר כְּדֵי שֶׁנּוּכַל לַעֲבוֹד עֲבוֹדָתֶךָ וְלִלְמוֹד תּוֹרָתֶךָ
כְּמוֹ שֶׁזַּנְתָּ לַאֲבוֹתֵינוּ מָן בַּמִּדְבָּר בְּאֶרֶץ צִיָּה וַעֲרָבָה:

פָּרָשַׁת הַמָּן

ד. וַיֹּאמֶר יְהוָֹה אֶל מֹשֶׁה, הִנְנִי מַמְטִיר לָכֶם
לֶחֶם מִן הַשָּׁמַיִם, וְיָצָא הָעָם וְלָקְטוּ דְּבַר יוֹם
בְּיוֹמוֹ, לְמַעַן אֲנַסֶּנּוּ הֲיֵלֵךְ בְּתוֹרָתִי אִם לֹא:
ה. וְהָיָה בַּיּוֹם הַשִּׁשִּׁי, וְהֵכִינוּ אֵת אֲשֶׁר יָבִיאוּ,
וְהָיָה מִשְׁנֶה, עַל אֲשֶׁר יִלְקְטוּ יוֹם יוֹם:
ו. וַיֹּאמֶר מֹשֶׁה וְאַהֲרֹן אֶל כָּל בְּנֵי יִשְׂרָאֵל,
עֶרֶב, וִידַעְתֶּם כִּי יְהוָֹה הוֹצִיא אֶתְכֶם מֵאֶרֶץ
מִצְרָיִם: ז. וּבֹקֶר, וּרְאִיתֶם אֶת כְּבוֹד יְהוָֹה,

The early authorities recommended reciting the Section of the Manna as a merit for a livelihood. (See Mishnah Berurah O.C. 1,5) Just as the Manna was food provided directly by Hashem, so too must one realize that although he toils and puts in effort, his livelihood ultimately comes from Hashem. Indeed, Hashem commanded Moshe to save a container of Manna for future generations to remind them that livelihood is in Hashem's hands.

Prayer before Parshas Hamaan

May there be the will before You, Hashem, our God and the God of our fathers that You prepare livelihood to all of Your nation the children of Israel. And include my livelihood and the livelihood of my household amongst them.

[May it come] with tranquility and not painfully, honorably and not with degradation, legally and not illegally, in order that we be able to do Your service and study Your Torah, just like You sustained our forefathers with Manna in the desert in a dry and barren land.

The Section of the Manna

4.   Then said Hashem to Moshe, Behold, I will rain bread from heaven for you; and the people shall go out and gather a set portion every day, that I may test[1] them, whether they will follow my law, or not:

5.   And it shall come to pass, that on the sixth day they shall prepare that which they bring in; and it shall be twice as much as they gather daily:

6.   And Moshe and Aaron said to all the people of Israel, "When evening arrives, you shall know that Hashem has brought you out from the land of Egypt:[2]

---

1. *They were tested to see if they would keep the special laws of the Manna ; not to leave over for the next day and not to gather on Shabbos.*
2. *In the evening they received meat which demonstrated that Hashem took them out of Egypt and had prepared for them food in the desert.*

בְּשָׁמְעוֹ אֶת תְּלֻנֹּתֵיכֶם עַל יְהֹוָה, וְנַחְנוּ מָה,
כִּי תַלִּינוּ עָלֵינוּ: ח. וַיֹּאמֶר מֹשֶׁה, בְּתֵת יְהֹוָה
לָכֶם בָּעֶרֶב בָּשָׂר לֶאֱכֹל, וְלֶחֶם בַּבֹּקֶר לִשְׂבֹּעַ,
בִּשְׁמֹעַ יְהֹוָה אֶת תְּלֻנֹּתֵיכֶם, אֲשֶׁר אַתֶּם
מַלִּינִם עָלָיו, וְנַחְנוּ מָה, לֹא עָלֵינוּ תְלֻנֹּתֵיכֶם,
כִּי עַל יְהֹוָה: ט. וַיֹּאמֶר מֹשֶׁה אֶל אַהֲרֹן, אֱמֹר
אֶל כָּל עֲדַת בְּנֵי יִשְׂרָאֵל, קִרְבוּ לִפְנֵי יְהֹוָה,
כִּי שָׁמַע אֵת תְּלֻנֹּתֵיכֶם: י. וַיְהִי כְּדַבֵּר אַהֲרֹן
אֶל כָּל עֲדַת בְּנֵי יִשְׂרָאֵל, וַיִּפְנוּ אֶל הַמִּדְבָּר,
וְהִנֵּה כְּבוֹד יְהֹוָה נִרְאָה בֶּעָנָן: יא. וַיְדַבֵּר יְהֹוָה
אֶל מֹשֶׁה לֵּאמֹר: יב. שָׁמַעְתִּי אֶת תְּלוּנֹת בְּנֵי
יִשְׂרָאֵל, דַּבֵּר אֲלֵהֶם לֵאמֹר, בֵּין הָעַרְבַּיִם
תֹּאכְלוּ בָשָׂר, וּבַבֹּקֶר תִּשְׂבְּעוּ לָחֶם, וִידַעְתֶּם
כִּי אֲנִי יְהֹוָה אֱלֹהֵיכֶם: יג. וַיְהִי בָעֶרֶב, וַתַּעַל
הַשְּׂלָו וַתְּכַס אֶת הַמַּחֲנֶה, וּבַבֹּקֶר הָיְתָה
שִׁכְבַת הַטַּל סָבִיב לַמַּחֲנֶה: יד. וַתַּעַל שִׁכְבַת
הַטָּל, וְהִנֵּה עַל פְּנֵי הַמִּדְבָּר דַּק מְחֻסְפָּס, דַּק
כַּכְּפֹר עַל הָאָרֶץ: טו. וַיִּרְאוּ בְנֵי יִשְׂרָאֵל,
וַיֹּאמְרוּ אִישׁ אֶל אָחִיו מָן הוּא, כִּי לֹא יָדְעוּ

7. And in the morning, then you shall see the glory of Hashem.[3] He hears your murmurings against Hashem[4]; and what are we, that you murmur against us:"

8. And Moshe said,[5] "When Hashem shall give you meat to eat in the evening, and in the morning bread to the full: Hashem hears your murmurings which you actually murmur against Him; and what are we? your murmurings are not against us, but against Hashem:"

9. And Moshe spoke to Aaron, "Say to all the congregation of the people of Israel, 'Come near before Hashem; for He has heard your murmurings:"

10. And it came to pass, as Aaron spoke to the whole congregation of the people of Israel, that they looked toward the desert, and, behold, the Glory of Hashem appeared in the cloud:

11. And Hashem spoke to Moshe, saying:

12. I have heard the murmurings of the people of Israel; speak to them, saying, At evening you shall eat meat, and in the morning you shall be filled with bread; and you shall know that I am Hashem your God:

13. And it came to pass, that at evening the quails came up, and covered the camp; and in the morning the dew lay around the camp:

14. And when the dew that lay evaporated, behold, upon the face of the desert there lay a fine revealed thing, as fine as frost on the ground:

15. And when the people of Israel saw it, they said one to another, "It is manna[6];" for they knew not what

---

3. *But the Manna which came in the morning showed not only that Hashem would provide for them but He provided in a loving fashion.*

4. *That which you complain to us, Hashem realizes that He is the point of your complaints.*

5. *This is in elaboration of the previous 2 verses.*

6. *A portion of food.*

מַה הוּא, וַיֹּאמֶר מֹשֶׁה אֲלֵיהֶם, הוּא הַלֶּחֶם
אֲשֶׁר נָתַן יְהוָֹה לָכֶם לְאָכְלָה: טז. זֶה הַדָּבָר
אֲשֶׁר צִוָּה יְהוָֹה, לִקְטוּ מִמֶּנּוּ אִישׁ לְפִי אָכְלוֹ,
עֹמֶר לַגֻּלְגֹּלֶת מִסְפַּר נַפְשֹׁתֵיכֶם, אִישׁ לַאֲשֶׁר
בְּאָהֳלוֹ תִּקָּחוּ: יז. וַיַּעֲשׂוּ כֵן בְּנֵי יִשְׂרָאֵל,
וַיִּלְקְטוּ הַמַּרְבֶּה וְהַמַּמְעִיט: יח. וַיָּמֹדּוּ בָעֹמֶר,
וְלֹא הֶעְדִּיף הַמַּרְבֶּה, וְהַמַּמְעִיט לֹא הֶחְסִיר,
אִישׁ לְפִי אָכְלוֹ לָקָטוּ: יט. וַיֹּאמֶר מֹשֶׁה אֲלֵהֶם,
אִישׁ אַל יוֹתֵר מִמֶּנּוּ עַד בֹּקֶר: כ. וְלֹא שָׁמְעוּ
אֶל מֹשֶׁה, וַיּוֹתִרוּ אֲנָשִׁים מִמֶּנּוּ עַד בֹּקֶר, וַיָּרֻם
תּוֹלָעִים וַיִּבְאַשׁ, וַיִּקְצֹף עֲלֵהֶם מֹשֶׁה:
כא. וַיִּלְקְטוּ אֹתוֹ בַּבֹּקֶר בַּבֹּקֶר, אִישׁ כְּפִי אָכְלוֹ,
וְחַם הַשֶּׁמֶשׁ וְנָמָס: כב. וַיְהִי בַּיּוֹם הַשִּׁשִּׁי, לָקְטוּ
לֶחֶם מִשְׁנֶה, שְׁנֵי הָעֹמֶר לָאֶחָד, וַיָּבֹאוּ כָּל
נְשִׂיאֵי הָעֵדָה וַיַּגִּידוּ לְמֹשֶׁה: כג. וַיֹּאמֶר אֲלֵהֶם,
הוּא אֲשֶׁר דִּבֶּר יְהוָֹה, שַׁבָּתוֹן שַׁבַּת קֹדֶשׁ
לַיהוָֹה מָחָר, אֵת אֲשֶׁר תֹּאפוּ אֵפוּ, וְאֵת אֲשֶׁר
תְּבַשְּׁלוּ בַּשֵּׁלוּ, וְאֵת כָּל הָעֹדֵף, הַנִּיחוּ לָכֶם
לְמִשְׁמֶרֶת עַד הַבֹּקֶר: כד. וַיַּנִּיחוּ אֹתוֹ עַד

it was; And Moshe said to them, "This is the bread which Hashem has given you to eat:"

16. This is what Hashem has commanded, "Gather of it every man according to his needs, an *omer* for every man, for the number of your persons[7]. Each of you shall take for the persons in his tent:

17. And the people of Israel did so, and gathered, some more, some less:

18. And when they did measure it with an *omer,* he who gathered much had nothing extra, and he who gathered little had no lack; they gathered every man according to his eating:

19. And Moshe said, "Let no man leave of it till the morning:"

20. However they listened not to Moshe; but some of them left of it until the morning, and it bred worms, and became putrid; and Moshe was angry with them:

21. And they gathered it every morning, every man according to his needs; and when the sun became hot, it melted:

22. And it came to pass, that on the sixth day they gathered twice as much bread, two *omers* for each man; and all the rulers of the congregation came and informed Moshe:

23. And he said to them, "This is what Hashem has said, 'Tomorrow is the Holy day of rest, the Sabbath to Hashem; bake that which you will bake today; and boil what you will boil, today; and that which remains, put away for safekeeping until the morning":

24. And they put it away till the morning, as Moshe bade; and it did not become putrid, nor were there any worms in it:

---

7. *An omer portion shall be taken for each member of the household.*

הַבֹּקֶר, כַּאֲשֶׁר צִוָּה מֹשֶׁה, וְלֹא הִבְאִישׁ, וְרִמָּה
לֹא הָיְתָה בּוֹ: כה. וַיֹּאמֶר מֹשֶׁה אִכְלֻהוּ הַיּוֹם,
כִּי שַׁבָּת הַיּוֹם לַיהוָה, הַיּוֹם לֹא תִמְצָאֻהוּ
בַּשָּׂדֶה: כו. שֵׁשֶׁת יָמִים תִּלְקְטֻהוּ, וּבַיּוֹם
הַשְּׁבִיעִי, שַׁבָּת לֹא יִהְיֶה בּוֹ: כז. וַיְהִי בַּיּוֹם
הַשְּׁבִיעִי, יָצְאוּ מִן הָעָם לִלְקֹט, וְלֹא מָצָאוּ:
כח. וַיֹּאמֶר יְהוָה אֶל מֹשֶׁה, עַד אָנָה מֵאַנְתֶּם,
לִשְׁמֹר מִצְוֹתַי וְתוֹרֹתָי: כט. רְאוּ כִּי יְהוָה נָתַן
לָכֶם הַשַּׁבָּת, עַל כֵּן הוּא נֹתֵן לָכֶם בַּיּוֹם
הַשִּׁשִּׁי לֶחֶם יוֹמָיִם, שְׁבוּ אִישׁ תַּחְתָּיו, אַל יֵצֵא
אִישׁ מִמְּקֹמוֹ בַּיּוֹם הַשְּׁבִיעִי: ל. וַיִּשְׁבְּתוּ הָעָם
בַּיּוֹם הַשְּׁבִיעִי: לא. וַיִּקְרְאוּ בֵית יִשְׂרָאֵל אֶת
שְׁמוֹ מָן, וְהוּא כְּזֶרַע גַּד לָבָן, וְטַעְמוֹ כְּצַפִּיחִת
בִּדְבָשׁ: לב. וַיֹּאמֶר מֹשֶׁה, זֶה הַדָּבָר אֲשֶׁר צִוָּה
יְהוָה, מְלֹא הָעֹמֶר מִמֶּנּוּ לְמִשְׁמֶרֶת לְדֹרֹתֵיכֶם,
לְמַעַן יִרְאוּ אֶת הַלֶּחֶם אֲשֶׁר הֶאֱכַלְתִּי אֶתְכֶם
בַּמִּדְבָּר, בְּהוֹצִיאִי אֶתְכֶם מֵאֶרֶץ מִצְרָיִם:
לג. וַיֹּאמֶר מֹשֶׁה אֶל אַהֲרֹן, קַח צִנְצֶנֶת אַחַת,
וְתֶן שָׁמָּה מְלֹא הָעֹמֶר מָן, וְהַנַּח אֹתוֹ לִפְנֵי

25. And Moshe said, "Eat it today; for today is a Sabbath to Hashem; today you shall not find it in the field:

26. Six days you shall gather it; but on the seventh day, which is the Sabbath, there shall be none":

27. And it came to pass that on the seventh day some of the people went out to gather, and they found none:

28. And Hashem said to Moshe, "How long refuse you to keep my commandments and my laws:

29. See, because Hashem has given you the Sabbath, therefore he gives you on the sixth day the bread of two days; abide you every man in his place, let ·no man go out of his place on the seventh day:"

30. The people rested on the seventh day:

31. And the house of Israel called its name Manna; and it was like coriander seed, white; and its taste was like wafers made with honey:

32. And Moshe said, "This is what Hashem commands[8], 'Fill an omer of it to be kept for your generations; that they may see the bread with which I have fed you in the wilderness, when I brought you out from the land of Egypt:'"

33. And Moshe said to Aaron, "Take a pot, and put an omer full of manna in it, and lay it up before Hashem, to be kept for your generations:"

---

8. *Hashem wanted later generations to realize that although they toil for a livelihood, ultimately their sustenance is in the hands of Hashem. Just as in the desert they were totally dependant on Him so too in the future we can rely only on Him.*

יְהוָֹה, לְמִשְׁמֶרֶת לְדֹרֹתֵיכֶם: לד. כַּאֲשֶׁר צִוָּה
יְהוָֹה אֶל מֹשֶׁה, וַיַּנִּיחֵהוּ אַהֲרֹן לִפְנֵי הָעֵדֻת
לְמִשְׁמָרֶת: לה. וּבְנֵי יִשְׂרָאֵל אָכְלוּ אֶת הַמָּן
אַרְבָּעִים שָׁנָה, עַד בֹּאָם אֶל אֶרֶץ נוֹשָׁבֶת, אֶת
הַמָּן אָכְלוּ עַד בֹּאָם אֶל קְצֵה אֶרֶץ כְּנָעַן:
לו. וְהָעֹמֶר, עֲשִׂרִית הָאֵיפָה הוּא:

34. As Hashem commanded Moshe, so Aaron laid it up before the Testimony, to be kept:

35. And the people of Israel ate manna forty years, until they came to inhabited land; they ate manna, until they came to the borders of the land of Canaan:

36. And an *omer* is the tenth part of an *ephah*:

תפלה אחר פרשת המן

אַתָּה הוּא יְהֹוָה לְבַדֶּךָ אַתָּה עָשִׂיתָ אֶת הַשָּׁמַיִם וּשְׁמֵי הַשָּׁמַיִם הָאָרֶץ וְכָל אֲשֶׁר עָלֶיהָ הַיַּמִּים וְכָל אֲשֶׁר בָּהֶם וְאַתָּה מְחַיֶּה אֶת כֻּלָּם וְאַתָּה הוּא שֶׁעָשִׂיתָ נִסִּים וְנִפְלָאוֹת גְּדוֹלוֹת תָּמִיד עִם אֲבוֹתֵינוּ גַּם בַּמִּדְבָּר הִמְטַרְתָּ לָהֶם לֶחֶם מִן הַשָּׁמַיִם וּמִצּוּר הַחַלָּמִישׁ הוֹצֵאתָ לָהֶם מַיִם וְגַם נָתַתָּ לָהֶם כָּל צָרְכֵיהֶם שִׂמְלוֹתָם לֹא בָלְתָה מֵעֲלֵיהֶם כֵּן בְּרַחֲמֶיךָ הָרַבִּים וּבַחֲסָדֶיךָ הָעֲצוּמִים תְּזוּנֵנוּ וּתְפַרְנְסֵנוּ וּתְכַלְכְּלֵנוּ וְתַסְפִּיק לָנוּ כָּל צָרְכֵנוּ וְצָרְכֵי עַמְּךָ בֵּית יִשְׂרָאֵל הַמְרוּבִּים בְּמִלּוּי וּבְרֶוַח בְּלִי טֹרַח וְעָמָל גָּדוֹל מִתַּחַת יָדְךָ הַנְּקִיָּה וְלֹא מִתַּחַת יְדֵי בָּשָׂר וָדָם:

יְהִי רָצוֹן מִלְּפָנֶיךָ יְהֹוָה אֱלֹהַי וֵאלֹהֵי אֲבוֹתַי שֶׁתָּכִין לִי וּלְאַנְשֵׁי בֵיתִי כָּל מַחֲסוֹרֵנוּ וְתַזְמִין לָנוּ כָּל צָרְכֵּנוּ לְכָל יוֹם וָיוֹם מֵחַיֵּינוּ דֵּי מַחֲסוֹרֵנוּ וּלְכָל שָׁעָה וְשָׁעָה מִשָּׁעוֹתֵינוּ דֵּי סִפּוּקֵנוּ וּלְכָל עֶצֶם מֵעֲצָמֵינוּ דֵּי מִחְיָתֵנוּ מִיָּדְךָ הַטּוֹבָה וְהָרְחָבָה וְלֹא כִּמְעוּט מִפְעָלֵינוּ וְקוֹצֶר חֲסָדֵינוּ וּמִזְעֵיר גְּמוּלוֹתֵינוּ וְיִהְיוּ מְזוֹנוֹתַי וּמְזוֹנוֹת אַנְשֵׁי בֵיתִי וְזַרְעִי וְזֶרַע זַרְעִי מְסוּרִים בְּיָדְךָ וְלֹא בְּיַד בָּשָׂר וָדָם:

Prayer after Parshas Hamaan

You alone are Hashem, You made the heavens and the high heavens, the earth and all that is upon it, the seas and all that is in them and You sustain them all. And You are the one who constantly did great wonders for our forefathers. Even in the desert You caused bread to fall from heaven like rain, and from the dry rock You brought out water, and You provided all their needs and their clothing did not wear out. So too with Your great mercy and loving kindness, feed and sustain us and provide all our needs and the needs of Your nation the children of Israel that are many. Fully and abundantly without inconvenience and great toil from beneath Your pure hand and not on account of flesh and blood.

May there be the will before you, Hashem, my God and the God of my forefathers, that you prepare for me and my household all that we are lacking, and you shall set aside for us all our needs. For each and every day of our lives provide that which we lack and for each hour of our lives prepare our provisions; for each bone in our bodies provide sustenance. As befitting Your great and benevolent hand and not in accordance with our humble actions and shallow kindness and lack of deeds. Let my livelihood and the livelihood of my household and progeny be placed in your hand and not in the hands of flesh and blood.

– 2 –

Tehillim for Gratitude

כוונות נכבדות למתפלל על הודאה

1) יכון שעיקר חפץ הקב"ה בהבריאה, הוא שהנבראים יודו לו שהוא בוראם וכל שיש להם בא מהמשי"ת.

2) יתן האדם הודאה שהקב"ה מחיה אותו בכל רגע כדכתיב בקרא השם נפשינו בחיים וכן כתיב כל הנשמה תהלל יה ופרשו חז"ל דעל כל נשימה ונשימה   יהלל להקב"ה.

3) אם נפל אדם בעת צרה וניצול או הגיע לו טובה גדולה יתן הודאה נוספת להקב"ה, ויחשוב דהצלתו או הטובה שהגיע לו הוא חסד הקב"ה עליו ולא מחמת זכויותיו. וטעם הדבר דבאמת נחשבנו כולנו חייבים. כמבואר בברכת הגומלים שמברכים הגומל לחייבים טובות.

4) הצלחת האדם הוא ע"י הארת פנים מאת הקב"ה. והרבה צרות נמצאים ע"י הסתרת פנים ח"ו. הדרך לזכות להארת פנים הוא ע"י הודאת תמידית להקב"ה. ומלבד ההודאה שיתן להקב"ה על ההצלה או על הטובה, יוסיף בעבודה כפי יכלתו במעשה מצוה בצדקה או בתפילה.

THOUGHTS BEFORE PRAYING IN GRATITUDE

1) The primary purpose that Hashem created this world is for His creations to acknowledge that He created them and that all they have come from Him.

2) One should praise Hashem when he realizes that Hashem is sustaining his life every second. This is expressed in the verse *"He who placed our souls amongst the living."* and in the verse *"All souls shall praise the Lord."* Our sages teach us that for every breath one must praise Hashem.

3) If one went through difficulties and was saved or he feels that he has been blessed with special favor or at a time of celebration, he must give added thanks to Hashem. He should realize that he was saved or granted favor only by the grace of Hashem and not because of his own merit, for in truth we are all guilty and undeserving.

4) Besides thanking Hashem for His salvation one should also increase his service of Hashem with concrete actions of Mitzvos, Charity and Prayer.

5) Man's success comes from the revelation of Hashem and hardship comes when Hashem hides His face. One merits the revelation of Hashem through constant acknowledgement of Hashem.

תהלים - ל

This Psalm was sung at the dedication of the Bais Hamikdash. It gives thanks to Hashem after recognizing all the travails which precede success.

א. מִזְמוֹר שִׁיר, חֲנֻכַּת הַבַּיִת לְדָוִד: ב. אֲרוֹמִמְךָ יְהֹוָה כִּי דִלִּיתָנִי, וְלֹא־שִׂמַּחְתָּ אֹיְבַי לִי: ג. יְהֹוָה אֱלֹהָי, שִׁוַּעְתִּי אֵלֶיךָ וַתִּרְפָּאֵנִי: ד. יְהֹוָה הֶעֱלִיתָ מִן־שְׁאוֹל נַפְשִׁי, חִיִּיתַנִי מִיָּרְדִי בוֹר: ה. זַמְּרוּ לַיהֹוָה חֲסִידָיו, וְהוֹדוּ לְזֵכֶר קָדְשׁוֹ: ו. כִּי רֶגַע בְּאַפּוֹ, חַיִּים בִּרְצוֹנוֹ, בָּעֶרֶב יָלִין בֶּכִי וְלַבֹּקֶר רִנָּה: ז. וַאֲנִי אָמַרְתִּי בְשַׁלְוִי, בַּל־אֶמּוֹט לְעוֹלָם: ח. יְהֹוָה בִּרְצוֹנְךָ הֶעֱמַדְתָּה לְהַרְרִי עֹז, הִסְתַּרְתָּ פָנֶיךָ הָיִיתִי נִבְהָל: ט. אֵלֶיךָ יְהֹוָה אֶקְרָא, וְאֶל־אֲדֹנָי אֶתְחַנָּן: י. מַה־בֶּצַע בְּדָמִי, בְּרִדְתִּי אֶל שַׁחַת, הֲיוֹדְךָ עָפָר, הֲיַגִּיד אֲמִתֶּךָ: יא. שְׁמַע־יְהֹוָה וְחָנֵּנִי, יְהֹוָה הֱיֵה־עֹזֵר לִי: יב. הָפַכְתָּ מִסְפְּדִי לְמָחוֹל לִי, פִּתַּחְתָּ שַׂקִּי וַתְּאַזְּרֵנִי שִׂמְחָה: יג. לְמַעַן יְזַמֶּרְךָ כָבוֹד וְלֹא יִדֹּם, יְהֹוָה אֱלֹהַי לְעוֹלָם אוֹדֶךָּ:

Psalm – 30

This Psalm was sung at the dedication of the Bais Hamikdash. It gives thanks to Hashem after recognizing all the travails which precede success.

1. A Psalm and Song of David; at the dedication of the House:

2. I will extol You, Hashem; for You have lifted me up, and have not made my enemies rejoice over me:

3. Hashem my God, I prayed to You, and you have healed me:

4. Hashem, You have brought up my soul from the grave; You have kept me alive, that I should not go down to the pit:

5. Sing to Hashem, O you His pious ones, and give thanks to His holy name:

6. For His anger lasts but a moment; in His favor is life; weeping may endure for a night, but joy comes in the morning:

7. And in my prosperity I said, I shall never be moved:

8. Hashem, by Your favor You have made stand as a strong mountain; You hid Your face, and I was frightened:

9. I cried to You, Hashem; and to Hashem I made supplication:

10. What profit is there in my blood, if I go down to the pit? Shall the dust praise You? Shall it declare Your truth?

11. Hear, Hashem, and be gracious to me; Hashem, be my helper:

12. You have turned for me my mourning into dancing; You have loosed my sackcloth, and girded me with gladness:

13. In order that my glory may sing praise to You, and not be silent; Hashem my God, I will give thanks to You forever:

תהלים – סו

This Psalm entreats the whole world to sing the praises of Hashem after recognizing all the kindness we receive from Him.

א. לַמְנַצֵּחַ שִׁיר מִזְמוֹר, הָרִיעוּ לֵאלֹהִים כָּל הָאָרֶץ: ב. זַמְּרוּ כְבוֹד־שְׁמוֹ, שִׂימוּ כָבוֹד תְּהִלָּתוֹ: ג. אִמְרוּ לֵאלֹהִים מַה־נּוֹרָא מַעֲשֶׂיךָ, בְּרֹב עֻזְּךָ, יְכַחֲשׁוּ לְךָ אֹיְבֶיךָ: ד. כָּל־הָאָרֶץ יִשְׁתַּחֲווּ לְךָ, וִיזַמְּרוּ־לָךְ, יְזַמְּרוּ שִׁמְךָ סֶלָה: ה. לְכוּ וּרְאוּ מִפְעֲלוֹת אֱלֹהִים, נוֹרָא עֲלִילָה עַל־בְּנֵי אָדָם: ו. הָפַךְ יָם לְיַבָּשָׁה, בַּנָּהָר יַעַבְרוּ בְרָגֶל, שָׁם נִשְׂמְחָה־בּוֹ: ז. מֹשֵׁל בִּגְבוּרָתוֹ עוֹלָם, עֵינָיו בַּגּוֹיִם תִּצְפֶּינָה, הַסּוֹרְרִים אַל־יָרִימוּ לָמוֹ סֶלָה: ח. בָּרְכוּ עַמִּים אֱלֹהֵינוּ, וְהַשְׁמִיעוּ קוֹל תְּהִלָּתוֹ: ט. הַשָּׂם נַפְשֵׁנוּ בַּחַיִּים, וְלֹא־נָתַן לַמּוֹט רַגְלֵנוּ: י. כִּי־בְחַנְתָּנוּ אֱלֹהִים, צְרַפְתָּנוּ כִּצְרָף־כָּסֶף: יא. הֲבֵאתָנוּ בַמְּצוּדָה, שַׂמְתָּ מוּעָקָה בְמָתְנֵינוּ: יב. הִרְכַּבְתָּ אֱנוֹשׁ לְרֹאשֵׁנוּ, בָּאנוּ־בָאֵשׁ וּבַמַּיִם, וַתּוֹצִיאֵנוּ לָרְוָיָה: יג. אָבוֹא בֵיתְךָ בְעוֹלוֹת, אֲשַׁלֵּם לְךָ נְדָרָי: יד. אֲשֶׁר־פָּצוּ שְׂפָתָי, וְדִבֶּר־פִּי בַּצַּר־לִי:

Psalm – 66

This Psalm entreats the whole world to sing the praises of Hashem after recognizing all the kindness we receive from Him.

1. To the chief Musician, A Song, a Psalm; Make a joyful noise to God, all the earth:

2. Sing to the honor of His name; make His praise glorious:

3. Say to God, "How awesome are your works"! Through the greatness of Your power shall Your enemies cringe before You:

4. All the earth shall bow to You, and shall sing to You; they shall sing to Your name; Selah:

5. Come and see the works of God; He is awesome in His doing toward the children of men:

6. He turned the sea into dry land; they passed through the river on foot; there did we rejoice in Him:

7. He rules by His power forever; His eyes behold the nations; let not the rebellious exalt themselves; Selah:

8. O bless our God, you peoples, and let the voice of His praise be heard:

9. Who has kept our soul among the living, and does not let our feet be moved:

10. For You, O God, have tested us; You have tried us, as silver is refined:

11. You have brought us into the net; You laid affliction upon our loins:

12. You have caused men to ride over our heads; we went through fire and through water; but You brought us out into abundance :

13. I will go into Your house with burnt offerings; I will pay You my vows:

14. Which my lips have uttered, and my mouth has spoken, when I was in trouble:

טו. עֲלוֹת מֵחִים אַעֲלֶה־לָּךְ עִם קְטֹרֶת אֵילִים, אֶעֱשֶׂה בָקָר עִם־עַתּוּדִים סֶלָה: טז. לְכוּ־שִׁמְעוּ וַאֲסַפְּרָה כָּל־יִרְאֵי אֱלֹהִים, אֲשֶׁר עָשָׂה לְנַפְשִׁי: יז. אֵלָיו פִּי־קָרָאתִי, וְרוֹמַם תַּחַת לְשׁוֹנִי: יח. אָוֶן אִם־רָאִיתִי בְלִבִּי, לֹא יִשְׁמַע אֲדֹנָי: יט. אָכֵן שָׁמַע אֱלֹהִים, הִקְשִׁיב בְּקוֹל תְּפִלָּתִי: כ. בָּרוּךְ אֱלֹהִים, אֲשֶׁר לֹא־הֵסִיר תְּפִלָּתִי וְחַסְדּוֹ מֵאִתִּי:

תהלים – צב

This Psalm declares our recognition of and thanks for all the good that Hashem does for us. Although at times it is difficult to see Hashem's good manifest in this world, with careful observation it can be seen.

א. מִזְמוֹר שִׁיר, לְיוֹם הַשַּׁבָּת: ב. טוֹב לְהֹדוֹת לַיהֹוָה, וּלְזַמֵּר לְשִׁמְךָ עֶלְיוֹן: ג. לְהַגִּיד בַּבֹּקֶר חַסְדֶּךָ, וֶאֱמוּנָתְךָ בַּלֵּילוֹת: ד. עֲלֵי־עָשׂוֹר וַעֲלֵי נָבֶל, עֲלֵי הִגָּיוֹן בְּכִנּוֹר: ה. כִּי שִׂמַּחְתַּנִי יְהֹוָה בְּפָעֳלֶךָ, בְּמַעֲשֵׂי יָדֶיךָ אֲרַנֵּן: ו. מַה־גָּדְלוּ מַעֲשֶׂיךָ יְהֹוָה, מְאֹד עָמְקוּ מַחְשְׁבֹתֶיךָ: ז. אִישׁ בַּעַר לֹא יֵדָע, וּכְסִיל לֹא־יָבִין אֶת־זֹאת: ח. בִּפְרֹחַ רְשָׁעִים כְּמוֹ עֵשֶׂב, וַיָּצִיצוּ כָּל־פֹּעֲלֵי אָוֶן לְהִשָּׁמְדָם עֲדֵי־עַד: ט. וְאַתָּה מָרוֹם לְעֹלָם

15. I will offer to you burnt sacrifices of fatlings, with the smoke of rams; I will offer bulls with goats; Selah:

16. Come and hear, all you who fear God, and I will declare what He has done for my soul:

17. I cried to Him with my mouth, and He was extolled with my tongue:

18. If I had looked on iniquity in my heart, Hashem would not have heard:

19. But truly God has heard me; He has attended to the voice of my prayer:

20. Blessed be God, Who has not rejected my prayer, nor removed His loving kindness from me:

Psalm – 92

This Psalm declares our recognition of and thanks for all the good that Hashem does for us. Although at times it is difficult to see Hashem's good manifest in this world, with careful observation it can be seen.

1. A Psalm Song for the Sabbath day:

2. It is a good thing to give thanks to Hashem, and to sing praises to Your name, O most high:

3. To declare Your loving kindness in the morning, and Your faithfulness every night:

4. Upon an instrument of ten strings, and upon the harp, to the melody of the lyre:

5. For You, Hashem, have made me glad through Your work; I will triumph in the works of Your hands:

6. Hashem, how great are Your works! And Your thoughts are very deep:

7. A stupid man does not know; nor can a fool understand this:

8. When the wicked spring like grass, and when all the evildoers flourish; it is that they shall be destroyed forever:

9. But You, Hashem, are most high for evermore:

יְהֹוָה: י. כִּי הִנֵּה אֹיְבֶיךָ יְהֹוָה, כִּי־הִנֵּה אֹיְבֶיךָ
יֹאבֵדוּ, יִתְפָּרְדוּ כָּל־פֹּעֲלֵי אָוֶן: יא. וַתָּרֶם
כִּרְאֵים קַרְנִי, בַּלֹּתִי בְּשֶׁמֶן רַעֲנָן: יב. וַתַּבֵּט עֵינִי
בְּשׁוּרָי, בַּקָּמִים עָלַי מְרֵעִים תִּשְׁמַעְנָה אָזְנָי:
יג. צַדִּיק כַּתָּמָר יִפְרָח, כְּאֶרֶז בַּלְּבָנוֹן יִשְׂגֶּה:
יד. שְׁתוּלִים בְּבֵית יְהֹוָה, בְּחַצְרוֹת אֱלֹהֵינוּ
יַפְרִיחוּ: טו. עוֹד יְנוּבוּן בְּשֵׂיבָה, דְּשֵׁנִים
וְרַעֲנַנִּים יִהְיוּ: טז. לְהַגִּיד כִּי־יָשָׁר יְהֹוָה, צוּרִי
וְלֹא־עַוְלָתָה בּוֹ:

תהלים – ק

*This Psalm was chanted in the Bais Hamikdash whenever a
Thanks Offering was brought.*

א. מִזְמוֹר לְתוֹדָה, הָרִיעוּ לַיהֹוָה כָּל־הָאָרֶץ:
ב. עִבְדוּ אֶת־יְהֹוָה בְּשִׂמְחָה, בֹּאוּ לְפָנָיו בִּרְנָנָה:
ג. דְּעוּ כִּי־יְהֹוָה הוּא אֱלֹהִים, הוּא־עָשָׂנוּ וְלוֹ
אֲנַחְנוּ, עַמּוֹ וְצֹאן מַרְעִיתוֹ: ד. בֹּאוּ שְׁעָרָיו
בְּתוֹדָה, חֲצֵרֹתָיו בִּתְהִלָּה הוֹדוּ־לוֹ בָּרְכוּ שְׁמוֹ:
ה. כִּי־טוֹב יְהֹוָה לְעוֹלָם חַסְדּוֹ, וְעַד־דֹּר וָדֹר
אֱמוּנָתוֹ:

10. For, behold, Your enemies, Hashem, for, behold, Your enemies shall perish; all the evildoers shall be scattered:

11. But You shall exalt my horn like the horn of a wild ox; I shall be anointed with fresh oil:

12. My eye has seen the downfall of my enemies, and my ears have heard the doom of the wicked who rise up against me:

13. The righteous will flourish like the palm tree; he will grow like a cedar in Lebanon:

14. Those that are planted in the house of Hashem shall flourish in the courts of our God:

15. They shall still bring forth fruit in old age; they shall be fat and flourishing:

16. To declare that Hashem is upright; He is my rock, and there is no iniquity in Him:

Psalm – 100

This Psalm was chanted in the Bais Hamikdash whenever a Thanks Offering was brought.

1. A Psalm of thanksgiving; Make a joyful noise to Hashem, all the earth:

2. Serve Hashem with gladness; come before His presence with singing:

3. Know that Hashem is God; it is He who made us, and we belong to Him; we are His people, and the sheep of His pasture:

4. Enter into His gates with thanksgiving, and into His courts with praise; be thankful to Him, and bless His name:

5. For Hashem is good; His loving kindness is everlasting; and his faithfulness endures to all generations:

תהלים – קז

This Psalm calls upon those whom have gone through a life threatening situation to proclaim their thanks. This brings one to comprehend all the kindness of Hashem.

א. הֹדוּ לַיהוָה כִּי־טוֹב, כִּי לְעוֹלָם חַסְדּוֹ:

ב. יֹאמְרוּ גְּאוּלֵי יְהוָה, אֲשֶׁר גְּאָלָם מִיַּד־צָר:

ג. וּמֵאֲרָצוֹת קִבְּצָם, מִמִּזְרָח וּמִמַּעֲרָב מִצָּפוֹן וּמִיָּם: ד. תָּעוּ בַמִּדְבָּר בִּישִׁימוֹן דָּרֶךְ, עִיר מוֹשָׁב לֹא מָצָאוּ: ה. רְעֵבִים גַּם־צְמֵאִים, נַפְשָׁם בָּהֶם תִּתְעַטָּף: ו. וַיִּצְעֲקוּ אֶל־יְהוָה בַּצַּר לָהֶם, מִמְּצוּקוֹתֵיהֶם יַצִּילֵם: ז. וַיַּדְרִיכֵם בְּדֶרֶךְ יְשָׁרָה, לָלֶכֶת אֶל־עִיר מוֹשָׁב: ח. יוֹדוּ לַיהוָה חַסְדּוֹ, וְנִפְלְאוֹתָיו לִבְנֵי אָדָם: ט. כִּי־הִשְׂבִּיעַ נֶפֶשׁ שֹׁקֵקָה, וְנֶפֶשׁ רְעֵבָה מִלֵּא־טוֹב: י. יֹשְׁבֵי חֹשֶׁךְ וְצַלְמָוֶת, אֲסִירֵי עֳנִי וּבַרְזֶל: יא. כִּי־הִמְרוּ אִמְרֵי־אֵל, וַעֲצַת עֶלְיוֹן נָאָצוּ: יב. וַיַּכְנַע בֶּעָמָל לִבָּם, כָּשְׁלוּ וְאֵין עֹזֵר: יג. וַיִּזְעֲקוּ אֶל־יְהוָה בַּצַּר לָהֶם, מִמְּצֻקוֹתֵיהֶם יוֹשִׁיעֵם: יד. יוֹצִיאֵם מֵחֹשֶׁךְ וְצַלְמָוֶת, וּמוֹסְרוֹתֵיהֶם יְנַתֵּק: טו. יוֹדוּ לַיהוָה חַסְדּוֹ,

Psalm – 107

This Psalm calls upon those whom have gone through a life threatening situation to proclaim their thanks. This brings one to comprehend all the kindness of Hashem.

1.   O give thanks to Hashem, for He is good; for his loving kindness endures for ever:

2.   Let the redeemed of Hashem say so, whom He has redeemed from the hand of the enemy:

3.   And gathered them from the lands, from the east, and from the west, from the north, and from the south:

4.   They wandered in the wilderness in a desert way; they found no city to dwell in:

5.   Hungry and thirsty, their soul fainted in them:

6.   Then they cried to Hashem in their trouble, and He saved them from their distresses:

7.   And He led them forth by the right way, that they might go to a city of habitation:

8.   Oh that men would praise Hashem for His loving kindness, and for His wonderful works to the children of men:

9.   For He satisfies the longing soul, and fills the hungry soul with goodness:

10.   Those who sit in darkness and in the shadow of death, bound in affliction and iron:

11.   Because they rebelled against the words of God, and rejected the counsel of the most High:

12.   And He brought down their heart with labor; they fell down, and there was none to help:

13.   Then they cried to Hashem in their trouble, and He saved them from their distresses:

14.   He brought them out of darkness and the shadow of death, and broke their bonds asunder:

15.   Let them praise Hashem for His loving kindness, and for His wonderful works to the children of men:

וְנִפְלְאוֹתָיו לִבְנֵי אָדָם: טז. כִּי־שִׁבַּר דַּלְתוֹת
נְחֹשֶׁת, וּבְרִיחֵי בַרְזֶל גִּדֵּעַ: יז. אֱוִלִים מִדֶּרֶךְ
פִּשְׁעָם, וּמֵעֲוֹנֹתֵיהֶם יִתְעַנּוּ: יח. כָּל־אֹכֶל תְּתַעֵב
נַפְשָׁם, וַיַּגִּיעוּ עַד־שַׁעֲרֵי מָוֶת: יט. וַיִּזְעֲקוּ אֶל־
יְהוָה בַּצַּר לָהֶם, מִמְּצֻקוֹתֵיהֶם יוֹשִׁיעֵם:
כ. יִשְׁלַח דְּבָרוֹ וְיִרְפָּאֵם, וִימַלֵּט מִשְּׁחִיתוֹתָם:
כא. יוֹדוּ לַיהוָה חַסְדּוֹ, וְנִפְלְאוֹתָיו לִבְנֵי אָדָם:
כב. וְיִזְבְּחוּ זִבְחֵי תוֹדָה, וִיסַפְּרוּ מַעֲשָׂיו בְּרִנָּה:
כג. יוֹרְדֵי הַיָּם בָּאֳנִיּוֹת, עֹשֵׂי מְלָאכָה בְּמַיִם
רַבִּים: כד. הֵמָּה רָאוּ מַעֲשֵׂי יְהוָה, וְנִפְלְאוֹתָיו
בִּמְצוּלָה: כה. וַיֹּאמֶר, וַיַּעֲמֵד רוּחַ סְעָרָה,
וַתְּרוֹמֵם גַּלָּיו: כו. יַעֲלוּ שָׁמַיִם יֵרְדוּ תְהוֹמוֹת,
נַפְשָׁם בְּרָעָה תִתְמוֹגָג: כז. יָחוֹגּוּ וְיָנוּעוּ
כַּשִּׁכּוֹר, וְכָל־חָכְמָתָם תִּתְבַּלָּע: כח. וַיִּצְעֲקוּ
אֶל־יְהוָה בַּצַּר לָהֶם, וּמִמְּצוּקֹתֵיהֶם יוֹצִיאֵם:
כט. יָקֵם סְעָרָה לִדְמָמָה, וַיֶּחֱשׁוּ גַּלֵּיהֶם:
ל. וַיִּשְׂמְחוּ כִי־יִשְׁתֹּקוּ, וַיַּנְחֵם אֶל־מְחוֹז חֶפְצָם:
לא. יוֹדוּ לַיהוָה חַסְדּוֹ, וְנִפְלְאוֹתָיו לִבְנֵי אָדָם:
לב. וִירֹמְמוּהוּ בִּקְהַל־עָם, וּבְמוֹשַׁב זְקֵנִים
יְהַלְלוּהוּ: לג. יָשֵׂם נְהָרוֹת לְמִדְבָּר, וּמֹצָאֵי מַיִם

16. For He broke the gates of bronze, and cut the bars of iron asunder:

17. Fools were afflicted because of their transgression, and because of their iniquities:

18. Their soul loathed all manner of food; and they came near to the gates of death:

19. Then they cried to Hashem in their trouble, and He saved them out of their distresses:

20. He sent his word, and healed them, and saved them from their destructions:

21. Let them praise Hashem for His loving kindness, and for His wonderful works to the children of men:

22. And let them sacrifice the sacrifices of thanksgiving, and declare His works with rejoicing:

23. Those who go down to the sea in ships, that do business in great waters:

24. Those saw the works of Hashem, and His wonders in the deep:

25. For He commands, and raises the stormy wind, which lifts up its waves:

26. They mount up to the sky, they go down again to the depths; their soul is melted because of trouble:

27. They reel to and fro, and stagger like a drunken man, and are at their wit's end:

28. Then they cry to Hashem in their trouble, and He brings them out of their distresses:

29. He calms the storm, so that its waves are still:

30. Then they are glad because they have quiet; and He brings them to their desired haven:

31. Let them praise Hashem for his loving kindness, and for His wonderful works to the children of men:

32. Let them exalt Him also in the congregation of the people, and praise Him in the assembly of the elders:

33. He turns rivers into a wilderness, and springs of water into dry ground:

לְצִמָּאוֹן: לד. אֶרֶץ פְּרִי לִמְלֵחָה, מֵרָעַת יֹשְׁבֵי
בָהּ: לה. יָשֵׂם מִדְבָּר לַאֲגַם־מַיִם, וְאֶרֶץ צִיָּה
לְמֹצָאֵי מָיִם: לו. וַיּוֹשֶׁב שָׁם רְעֵבִים, וַיְכוֹנְנוּ
עִיר מוֹשָׁב: לז. וַיִּזְרְעוּ שָׂדוֹת וַיִּטְּעוּ כְרָמִים,
וַיַּעֲשׂוּ פְּרִי תְבוּאָה: לח. וַיְבָרֲכֵם וַיִּרְבּוּ מְאֹד,
וּבְהֶמְתָּם לֹא יַמְעִיט: לט. וַיִּמְעֲטוּ וַיָּשֹׁחוּ,
מֵעֹצֶר רָעָה וְיָגוֹן: מ. שֹׁפֵךְ בּוּז עַל־נְדִיבִים,
וַיַּתְעֵם בְּתֹהוּ לֹא־דָרֶךְ: מא. וַיְשַׂגֵּב אֶבְיוֹן
מֵעוֹנִי, וַיָּשֶׂם כַּצֹּאן מִשְׁפָּחוֹת: מב. יִרְאוּ
יְשָׁרִים וְיִשְׂמָחוּ, וְכָל־עַוְלָה קָפְצָה פִּיהָ: מג. מִי
חָכָם וְיִשְׁמָר־אֵלֶּה, וְיִתְבּוֹנְנוּ חַסְדֵי יְהוָה:

תהלים – קיא

This Psalm proclaims acknowledgement of Hashems deeds, that His works are great and He provides for all.

א. הַלְלוּיָהּ, אוֹדֶה יְהוָה בְּכָל־לֵבָב, בְּסוֹד
יְשָׁרִים וְעֵדָה: ב. גְּדֹלִים מַעֲשֵׂי יְהוָה, דְּרוּשִׁים
לְכָל־חֶפְצֵיהֶם: ג. הוֹד־וְהָדָר פָּעֳלוֹ, וְצִדְקָתוֹ
עֹמֶדֶת לָעַד: ד. זֵכֶר עָשָׂה לְנִפְלְאֹתָיו, חַנּוּן
וְרַחוּם יְהוָה: ה. טֶרֶף נָתַן לִירֵאָיו, יִזְכֹּר לְעוֹלָם

34. A fruitful land into barrenness, because of the wickedness of its inhabitants:

35. He turns the wilderness into a pool of water, and dry ground into springs of water:

36. And there He lets the hungry dwell, and they establish a city for habitation:

37. And sow the fields, and plant vineyards, which get a fruitful yield:

38. And He blesses them, so that they are multiplied greatly; and does not let their cattle decrease:

39. When they are diminished and brought low through oppression, affliction, and sorrow:

40. He pours contempt upon nobles, and causes them to wander in the wilderness, where there is no way:

41. But He raises the poor high out of affliction, and makes his families like a flock:

42. The righteous shall see it, and rejoice; and all iniquity shall shut its mouth:

43. Whoever is wise, and will observe these things, let them consider the loving kindness of Hashem:

Psalm – 111

This Psalm proclaims acknowledgement of Hashems deeds, that His works are great and He provides for all.

1. Halleluyah! I will praise Hashem with my whole heart, in the assembly of the upright, and in the congregation:

2. The works of Hashem are great, sought out all by all who love them:

3. His work is honorable and glorious; and His righteousness endures forever:

4. He has made His wonderful works to be remembered; Hashem is gracious and full of compassion:

5. He has given food to those who fear Him; He is ever

בְּרִיתוֹ: ו. כֹּחַ מַעֲשָׂיו הִגִּיד לְעַמּוֹ, לָתֵת לָהֶם
נַחֲלַת גּוֹיִם: ז. מַעֲשֵׂי יָדָיו אֱמֶת וּמִשְׁפָּט,
נֶאֱמָנִים כָּל־פִּקּוּדָיו: ח. סְמוּכִים לָעַד לְעוֹלָם,
עֲשׂוּיִם בֶּאֱמֶת וְיָשָׁר: ט. פְּדוּת שָׁלַח לְעַמּוֹ,
צִוָּה־לְעוֹלָם בְּרִיתוֹ, קָדוֹשׁ וְנוֹרָא שְׁמוֹ:
י. רֵאשִׁית חָכְמָה יִרְאַת יְהֹוָה, שֵׂכֶל טוֹב לְכָל־
עֹשֵׂיהֶם, תְּהִלָּתוֹ עֹמֶדֶת לָעַד:

תהלים - קנ

This Psalm declares that we must praise Hashem with all our faculties.

א. הַלְלוּיָהּ, הַלְלוּ־אֵל בְּקָדְשׁוֹ, הַלְלוּהוּ בִּרְקִיעַ
עֻזּוֹ: ב. הַלְלוּהוּ בִגְבוּרֹתָיו, הַלְלוּהוּ כְּרֹב גֻּדְלוֹ:
ג. הַלְלוּהוּ בְּתֵקַע שׁוֹפָר, הַלְלוּהוּ בְּנֵבֶל וְכִנּוֹר:
ד. הַלְלוּהוּ בְּתֹף וּמָחוֹל, הַלְלוּהוּ בְּמִנִּים וְעוּגָב:
ה. הַלְלוּהוּ בְצִלְצְלֵי־שָׁמַע, הַלְלוּהוּ בְּצִלְצְלֵי
תְרוּעָה: ו. כֹּל הַנְּשָׁמָה תְּהַלֵּל יָהּ, הַלְלוּיָהּ:

74

mindful of His covenant:

6. He has declared to His people the power of His works, that He may give them the heritage of the nations:

7. The works of His hands are truth and justice; all His commandments are sure:

8. They stand fast forever and ever, and are done in truth and uprightness:

9. He sent redemption to His people; He has commanded His covenant forever; holy and reverend is His name:

10. The fear of Hashem is the beginning of wisdom; a good understanding have all those who do His commandments; His praise endures forever:

Psalm – 150

This Psalm declares that we must praise Hashem with all our faculties.

1. Halleluyah! Praise God in His sanctuary! Praise Him in the firmament of His power:

2. Praise Him for His mighty acts! Praise Him according to His exceeding greatness:

3. Praise Him with the sound of the shofar! Praise Him with the harp and the lyre:

4. Praise Him with the tambourine and dance! Praise Him with stringed instruments and the pipe:

5. Praise Him with sounding cymbals! Praise Him with loud clashing cymbals:

6. Let every thing that breathes praise Hashem! Halleluyah:

תהילים לחתונה

תהלים – יט

This Psalm relates that Hashem can be seen through the forces and order of nature. But ultimately the true recognition and acceptance of Hashem is through the revelation of the Torah at Sinai. The sun which is one of the great forces of nature is compared to the groom emerging from his bridal chamber.

א. לַמְנַצֵּחַ מִזְמוֹר לְדָוִד: ב. הַשָּׁמַיִם מְסַפְּרִים כְּבוֹד־אֵל, וּמַעֲשֵׂה יָדָיו מַגִּיד הָרָקִיעַ: ג. יוֹם לְיוֹם יַבִּיעַ אֹמֶר, וְלַיְלָה לְּלַיְלָה יְחַוֶּה־דָּעַת: ד. אֵין־אֹמֶר וְאֵין דְּבָרִים, בְּלִי נִשְׁמָע קוֹלָם: ה. בְּכָל־הָאָרֶץ יָצָא קַוָּם, וּבִקְצֵה תֵבֵל מִלֵּיהֶם, לַשֶּׁמֶשׁ שָׂם־אֹהֶל בָּהֶם: ו. וְהוּא כְּחָתָן יֹצֵא מֵחֻפָּתוֹ, יָשִׂישׂ כְּגִבּוֹר לָרוּץ אֹרַח: ז. מִקְצֵה הַשָּׁמַיִם מוֹצָאוֹ, וּתְקוּפָתוֹ עַל־קְצוֹתָם, וְאֵין נִסְתָּר מֵחַמָּתוֹ: ח. תּוֹרַת יהוה תְּמִימָה, מְשִׁיבַת נָפֶשׁ, עֵדוּת יהוה נֶאֱמָנָה מַחְכִּימַת פֶּתִי: ט. פִּקּוּדֵי יהוה יְשָׁרִים, מְשַׂמְּחֵי לֵב, מִצְוַת יהוה בָּרָה, מְאִירַת עֵינָיִם: י. יִרְאַת יהוה טְהוֹרָה, עוֹמֶדֶת לָעַד, מִשְׁפְּטֵי־יהוה אֱמֶת צָדְקוּ יַחְדָּו: יא. הַנֶּחֱמָדִים מִזָּהָב וּמִפַּז רָב,

Psalms to be recited for a Wedding

Psalm – 19

This Psalm relates that Hashem can be seen through the forces and order of nature. But ultimately the true recognition and acceptance of Hashem is through the revelation of the Torah at Sinai. The sun which is one of the great forces of nature is compared to the groom emerging from his bridal chamber.

1. To the chief Musician, A Psalm of David:

2. The heavens declare the glory of God; and the firmament proclaims His handiwork:

3. Day to day utters speech, and night to night expresses[1] knowledge:

4. There is no speech nor are there any words; their voice is not heard:

5. Their line[2] is gone out through all the earth, and their words to the end of the world; In them He has set a tent for the sun:

6. Which comes forth like a bridegroom leaving his chamber, and rejoices like a strong man when he runs a race:

7. His going forth is from the end of the heaven, and his circuit to the ends of it; and there is nothing hidden from his heat:

8. The Torah of Hashem is perfect, reviving the soul; the testimony of Hashem is sure, making wise the simple:

9. The statutes of Hashem are right, rejoicing the heart; the commandment of Hashem is pure, enlightening the eyes:

10. The fear of Hashem is pure, enduring forever; the judgments of Hashem are true and righteous altogether:

11. More to be desired are they than gold, even very fine

---

1. *When one watches the constant rising and setting of the sun it induces one to speak about the praises of Hashem.*
2. *This refers to the path of the sun.*

וּמְתוּקִים מִדְּבַשׁ וְנֹפֶת צוּפִים: יב. גַּם־עַבְדְּךָ
נִזְהָר בָּהֶם, בְּשָׁמְרָם עֵקֶב רָב: יג. שְׁגִיאוֹת מִי
יָבִין, מִנִּסְתָּרוֹת נַקֵּנִי: יד. גַּם מִזֵּדִים חֲשֹׂךְ
עַבְדֶּךָ, אַל־יִמְשְׁלוּ־בִי אָז אֵיתָם, וְנִקֵּיתִי
מִפֶּשַׁע רָב: טו. יִהְיוּ לְרָצוֹן אִמְרֵי־פִי, וְהֶגְיוֹן
לִבִּי לְפָנֶיךָ, יהוה צוּרִי וְגֹאֲלִי:

תהלים – קלג

When Jews are united in brotherhood Hashem's blessings will flow like a stream.

א. שִׁיר הַמַּעֲלוֹת לְדָוִד, הִנֵּה מַה־טּוֹב וּמַה
נָּעִים, שֶׁבֶת אַחִים גַּם־יָחַד: ב. כַּשֶּׁמֶן הַטּוֹב עַל
הָרֹאשׁ, יֹרֵד עַל־הַזָּקָן, זְקַן־אַהֲרֹן, שֶׁיֹּרֵד עַל־
פִּי מִדּוֹתָיו: ג. כְּטַל־חֶרְמוֹן שֶׁיֹּרֵד עַל־הַרְרֵי
צִיּוֹן, כִּי שָׁם צִוָּה יְהֹוָה אֶת־הַבְּרָכָה, חַיִּים עַד
הָעוֹלָם:

gold; sweeter also than honey and the honeycomb:

12. Moreover by them is your servant warned; and in keeping of them there is great reward:

13. Who can discern his errors? Clean me from hidden faults:

14. Keep back Your servant also from presumptuous sins; let them not have dominion over me; then shall I be blameless, and innocent of great transgression:

15. Let the words of my mouth, and the meditation of my heart, be acceptable before you, Hashem, my rock, and my redeemer:

Psalm – 133

When Jews are united in brotherhood Hashem's blessings will flow like a stream.

1. A Song of Ascents of David; Behold, how good and how pleasant it is for brothers to dwell together in unity:

2. It is like the precious ointment upon the head, that runs down upon[1] the beard, Aaron's beard, that runs down to the hem of his garments:

3. Like the dew of Hermon descending upon the mountains of Zion; for there Hashem has commanded the blessing, life for evermore:

---

1. *This is an allegory to the oil of anointment that was poured liberally until it ran down his beard and onto his garment.*

תהלים - קכח

When one follows honestly in the ways of Hashem he will experience
success in this world. His home will be blessed with a good hearted wife
and children.

א. שִׁיר הַמַּעֲלוֹת, אַשְׁרֵי כָּל־יְרֵא יְהוָה, הַהֹלֵךְ בִּדְרָכָיו: ב. יְגִיעַ כַּפֶּיךָ כִּי תֹאכֵל, אַשְׁרֶיךָ וְטוֹב לָךְ: ג. אֶשְׁתְּךָ כְּגֶפֶן פֹּרִיָּה, בְּיַרְכְּתֵי בֵיתֶךָ, בָּנֶיךָ כִּשְׁתִלֵי זֵיתִים, סָבִיב לְשֻׁלְחָנֶךָ: ד. הִנֵּה כִי־כֵן יְבֹרַךְ גָּבֶר, יְרֵא יְהוָה: ה. יְבָרֶכְךָ יְהוָה מִצִּיּוֹן, וּרְאֵה בְּטוּב יְרוּשָׁלָם, כֹּל יְמֵי חַיֶּיךָ: ו. וּרְאֵה בָנִים לְבָנֶיךָ, שָׁלוֹם עַל־יִשְׂרָאֵל:

תהלים - קכז

Although one must toil to provide for himself, house and home; success
will come only through divine help.

א. שִׁיר הַמַּעֲלוֹת לִשְׁלֹמֹה, אִם־יְהוָה לֹא־יִבְנֶה בַיִת, שָׁוְא עָמְלוּ בוֹנָיו בּוֹ, אִם־יְהוָה לֹא־יִשְׁמָר עִיר, שָׁוְא שָׁקַד שׁוֹמֵר: ב. שָׁוְא לָכֶם מַשְׁכִּימֵי קוּם מְאַחֲרֵי־שֶׁבֶת, אֹכְלֵי לֶחֶם הָעֲצָבִים, כֵּן יִתֵּן לִידִידוֹ שֵׁנָא: ג. הִנֵּה נַחֲלַת יְהוָה בָּנִים, שָׂכָר פְּרִי הַבָּטֶן: ד. כְּחִצִּים בְּיַד־גִּבּוֹר, כֵּן בְּנֵי

Psalm – 128

When one follows honestly in the ways of Hashem he will experience success in this world. His home will be blessed with a good hearted wife and children.

1. A Song of Ascents; Happy is every one who fears Hashem; who walks in his ways:

2. For you shall eat the labor of your hands; happy shall you be, and it shall be well with you:

3. Your wife shall be like a fruitful vine in the recesses of your house; your children like olive shoots around your table:

4. Behold, thus shall the man be blessed who fears Hashem:

5. Hashem shall bless you from Zion; and you shall see the good of Jerusalem all the days of your life:

6. And you shall see your children's children, and peace upon Israel:

Psalm – 127

Although one must toil to provide for himself, house and home; success will come only through divine help.

1. A Song of Ascents for Solomon; Unless Hashem builds the house, those who build it labor in vain; unless Hashem watches over the city, the watchman stays awake in vain:

2. It is vain for you to rise up early, to sit up late, to eat the bread of toil; for truly to his beloved he gives sleep:[1]

3. Behold, children are a heritage of Hashem; and the fruit of the womb is a reward:

4. As arrows are in the hand of a mighty man; so are the children of one's youth:

---

1. *One who Hashem shows favor to will make a living and still be able to sleep at night.*

הַנְּעוּרִים: ה. אַשְׁרֵי הַגֶּבֶר אֲשֶׁר מִלֵּא אֶת אַשְׁפָּתוֹ מֵהֶם, לֹא־יֵבֹשׁוּ כִּי־יְדַבְּרוּ אֶת־אוֹיְבִים בַּשָּׁעַר:

5.   Happy is the man who has his quiver full of them; they shall not be put to shame, but they shall speak with the enemies in the gate:

תהילים ליולדת

תהלים - כ

This Psalm declares that Hashem will answer those who call to him in times of distress.

א. לַמְנַצֵּחַ, מִזְמוֹר לְדָוִד: ב. יַעַנְךָ יְהוָה בְּיוֹם צָרָה, יְשַׂגֶּבְךָ שֵׁם אֱלֹהֵי יַעֲקֹב: ג. יִשְׁלַח עֶזְרְךָ מִקֹּדֶשׁ, וּמִצִּיּוֹן יִסְעָדֶךָ: ד. יִזְכֹּר כָּל־מִנְחֹתֶיךָ, וְעוֹלָתְךָ יְדַשְּׁנֶה סֶלָה: ה. יִתֶּן־לְךָ כִלְבָבֶךָ, וְכָל־עֲצָתְךָ יְמַלֵּא: ו. נְרַנְּנָה בִּישׁוּעָתֶךָ וּבְשֵׁם אֱלֹהֵינוּ נִדְגֹּל, יְמַלֵּא יְהוָה כָּל־מִשְׁאֲלוֹתֶיךָ: ז. עַתָּה יָדַעְתִּי כִּי הוֹשִׁיעַ יְהוָה מְשִׁיחוֹ, יַעֲנֵהוּ מִשְּׁמֵי קָדְשׁוֹ, בִּגְבֻרוֹת יֵשַׁע יְמִינוֹ: ח. אֵלֶּה בָרֶכֶב וְאֵלֶּה בַסּוּסִים, וַאֲנַחְנוּ בְּשֵׁם־יְהוָה אֱלֹהֵינוּ נַזְכִּיר: ט. הֵמָּה כָּרְעוּ וְנָפָלוּ, וַאֲנַחְנוּ קַמְנוּ וַנִּתְעוֹדָד: י. יְהוָה הוֹשִׁיעָה, הַמֶּלֶךְ יַעֲנֵנוּ בְיוֹם־קָרְאֵנוּ:

Psalm to be recited during Childbirth

Psalm – 20

This Psalm declares that Hashem will answer those who call to him in times of distress.

1. To the chief Musician, A Psalm of David:

2. May Hashem hear you in the day of trouble! May the Name of the God of Jacob defend you:

3. May He send you help from the sanctuary, and strengthen you out of Zion:

4. May He remember all your offerings, and accept with favor your burnt sacrifice! Selah:

5. May He grant you your heart's desire, and fulfil all your plans:

6. May we rejoice in Your salvation, and in the name of our God set up our banners! May Hashem fulfil all your petitions:

7. Now I know that Hashem saves His anointed; He will answer him from His holy heaven with the saving strength of His right hand:

8. Some trust in chariots, and some in horses; but we will mention the Name of Hashem our God:

9. They are brought down and fall; but we shall rise, and stand upright:

10. Hashem, please save. The king will answer us on the day when we call:

תהילים למילה

תהלים - יב

*One must place his trust in Hashem not in people. This Psalm was said
by David in honor of the mitzvah of Bris which is performed on the
eighth day.*

א. לַמְנַצֵּחַ עַל־הַשְּׁמִינִית, מִזְמוֹר לְדָוִד:
ב. הוֹשִׁיעָה יהוה כִּי־גָמַר חָסִיד, כִּי־פַסּוּ
אֱמוּנִים מִבְּנֵי אָדָם: ג. שָׁוְא יְדַבְּרוּ אִישׁ אֶת
רֵעֵהוּ, שְׂפַת חֲלָקוֹת, בְּלֵב וָלֵב יְדַבֵּרוּ: ד. יַכְרֵת
יהוה כָּל־שִׂפְתֵי חֲלָקוֹת, לָשׁוֹן מְדַבֶּרֶת גְּדֹלוֹת:
ה. אֲשֶׁר אָמְרוּ לִלְשֹׁנֵנוּ נַגְבִּיר, שְׂפָתֵינוּ אִתָּנוּ,
מִי אָדוֹן לָנוּ: ו. מִשֹּׁד עֲנִיִּים, מֵאַנְקַת אֶבְיוֹנִים,
עַתָּה אָקוּם יֹאמַר יהוה, אָשִׁית בְּיֵשַׁע יָפִיחַ
לוֹ: ז. אִמְרוֹת יהוה, אֲמָרוֹת טְהֹרוֹת, כֶּסֶף
צָרוּף בַּעֲלִיל לָאָרֶץ, מְזֻקָּק שִׁבְעָתָיִם: ח. אַתָּה
יהוה תִּשְׁמְרֵם, תִּצְּרֶנּוּ מִן־הַדּוֹר זוּ לְעוֹלָם:
ט. סָבִיב רְשָׁעִים יִתְהַלָּכוּן, כְּרֻם זֻלּוּת לִבְנֵי
אָדָם:

86

This Psalm is recited at Bris Milah

Psalm – 12

One must place his trust in Hashem not in people. This Psalm was said by David in honor of the mitzvah of Bris which is performed on the eighth day.

1. To the chief Musician, according to the Sheminith[1], A Psalm of David:

2. Help Hashem, for the pious man ceases; for the faithful vanish from among the children of men:

3. They speak vanity every one with his neighbor; with flattering lips and with a double heart they speak:

4. Hashem shall cut off all flattering lips, and the tongue that speaks arrogant things:

5. Who have said, "With our tongue we will prevail; our lips are our own; who is lord over us:"

6. For the oppression of the poor, for the sighing of the needy, now will I arise, said Hashem; I will set him in safety at whom they hiss:

7. The words of Hashem are pure words; like silver refined in a furnace upon the ground, purified seven times:

8. You shall keep them, Hashem, you shall preserve them from this generation forever:

9. The wicked walk on every side, when vileness is exalted among the son of men:

---

1. *An eight stringed instrument. Our sages tell us that this Psalm was dedicated to Bris Milah which is performed on the eighth day.*

– 3 –

Tehillim for Repentance

כוונות נכבדות למתפלל על תשובה

1) יש סייעתא דשמיא מיוחדת לסייע האדם לעשות תשובה, ואין חטא בעולם שאין עליו תשובה.

2) ענין גדול הוא להתפלל שהקב״ה יעזור לו שיעשה תשובה. ותפילה מועילה שיתרבה הסיוע מאת הקב״ה שיעשה תשובה.

3) אף מי שאין לבו שלם לעשות תשובה מ״מ אם יתפלל שהקב״ה יעזור לו, יועיל שהקב״ה יתן לו הכח לעזוב החטא ולעשות תשובה.

4) יאמין שבזכות התפילה על התשובה ועל קידוש שם שמים יצמח הגאולה ויתגלה השכינה.

THOUGHTS BEFORE PRAYING FOR REPENTANCE

1) There is special Divine inspiration to help one to repent. There is no sin that is beyond repentance.

2) It is of great importance to ask Hashem to help one to repent. This prayer will cause a greater divine inspiration to help one.

3) If one prays that Hashem help him repent, then even if he was not genuinely committed to repent, Hashem will give him the strength to abandon his sin and repent.

4) The final redemption will sprout forth and the Divine Presence will be revealed through our prayers to return to Hashem and sanctify His Name.

תהלים ו

This Psalm is said in the Tachanun prayer. We acknowledge that we have sinned and are deserving of life only by Divine grace.

א. לַמְנַצֵּחַ בִּנְגִינוֹת, עַל הַשְּׁמִינִית מִזְמוֹר לְדָוִד: ב. יְהוָה אַל־בְּאַפְּךָ תוֹכִיחֵנִי, וְאַל בַּחֲמָתְךָ תְיַסְּרֵנִי: ג. חָנֵּנִי יְהוָה כִּי אֻמְלַל אָנִי, רְפָאֵנִי יְהוָה כִּי נִבְהֲלוּ עֲצָמָי: ד. וְנַפְשִׁי נִבְהֲלָה מְאֹד, וְאַתָּה יְהוָה עַד־מָתָי: ה. שׁוּבָה יְהוָה חַלְּצָה נַפְשִׁי, הוֹשִׁיעֵנִי לְמַעַן חַסְדֶּךָ: ו. כִּי אֵין בַּמָּוֶת זִכְרֶךָ, בִּשְׁאוֹל מִי יוֹדֶה־לָּךְ: ז. יָגַעְתִּי בְּאַנְחָתִי, אַשְׂחֶה בְכָל־לַיְלָה מִטָּתִי, בְּדִמְעָתִי עַרְשִׂי אַמְסֶה: ח. עָשְׁשָׁה מִכַּעַס עֵינִי, עָתְקָה בְּכָל־צוֹרְרָי: ט. סוּרוּ מִמֶּנִּי כָּל־פֹּעֲלֵי אָוֶן, כִּי־שָׁמַע יְהוָה קוֹל בִּכְיִי: י. שָׁמַע יְהוָה תְּחִנָּתִי, יְהוָה תְּפִלָּתִי יִקָּח: יא. יֵבֹשׁוּ וְיִבָּהֲלוּ מְאֹד כָּל־אֹיְבָי, יָשֻׁבוּ יֵבֹשׁוּ רָגַע:

---

2. When wicked repent they will be ashamed only for an instant because after their repentance is accepted, Hashem treats them as if they have never sinned and their shame will not continue.

Psalm – 6

This Psalm is said in the Tachanun prayer. We acknowledge that we have sinned and are deserving of life only by Divine grace.

1. To the chief Musician for stringed instruments, according to the Sheminith, a psalm of David:

2. Hashem, do not rebuke me in your anger, nor chasten me in your hot displeasure:

3. Have mercy upon me, Hashem; for I am weak; Hashem, heal me; for my bones shudder:

4. My soul is also much troubled; And You, Hashem, how long:?[1]

5. Return, Hashem, deliver my soul; Oh save me for the sake of Your loving kindness:

6. For in death there is no remembrance of You; In the grave who shall give You thanks:

7. I am weary with my moaning; all night I make my bed swim; I drench my couch with my tears:

8. My eye wastes away because of grief; it grows weak because of all my enemies:

9. Depart from me, all you evildoers; for Hashem has heard the voice of my weeping:

10. Hashem has heard my supplication; Hashem will receive my prayer:

11. Let all my enemies be ashamed and be much troubled; let them return and be ashamed in a moment:[2]

---

1. *Will you see my affliction and not heal me? Rashi, Radak.*

תהלים – כה

In this Psalm one acknowledges his sin and begs to be taught the way to come close to Hashem.

א. לְדָוִד, אֵלֶיךָ יהוה נַפְשִׁי אֶשָּׂא: ב. אֱלֹהַי בְּךָ
בָטַחְתִּי אַל־אֵבוֹשָׁה, אַל־יַעַלְצוּ אֹיְבַי לִי: ג. גַּם
כָּל־קֹוֶיךָ לֹא יֵבֹשׁוּ, יֵבֹשׁוּ הַבּוֹגְדִים רֵיקָם:
ד. דְּרָכֶיךָ יהוה הוֹדִיעֵנִי, אֹרְחוֹתֶיךָ לַמְּדֵנִי:
ה. הַדְרִיכֵנִי בַאֲמִתֶּךָ, וְלַמְּדֵנִי, כִּי־אַתָּה אֱלֹהֵי
יִשְׁעִי, אוֹתְךָ קִוִּיתִי כָּל־הַיּוֹם: ו. זְכֹר־רַחֲמֶיךָ
יהוה, וַחֲסָדֶיךָ, כִּי מֵעוֹלָם הֵמָּה: ז. חַטֹּאות
נְעוּרַי וּפְשָׁעַי אַל־תִּזְכֹּר, כְּחַסְדְּךָ זְכָר־לִי־
אַתָּה, לְמַעַן טוּבְךָ יהוה: ח. טוֹב־וְיָשָׁר יהוה,
עַל־כֵּן יוֹרֶה חַטָּאִים בַּדָּרֶךְ: ט. יַדְרֵךְ עֲנָוִים
בַּמִּשְׁפָּט, וִילַמֵּד עֲנָוִים דַּרְכּוֹ: י. כָּל־אָרְחוֹת
יהוה חֶסֶד וֶאֱמֶת, לְנֹצְרֵי בְרִיתוֹ וְעֵדֹתָיו:
יא. לְמַעַן־שִׁמְךָ יהוה, וְסָלַחְתָּ לַעֲוֹנִי כִּי רַב־
הוּא: יב. מִי־זֶה הָאִישׁ יְרֵא יהוה, יוֹרֶנּוּ בְּדֶרֶךְ
יִבְחָר: יג. נַפְשׁוֹ בְּטוֹב תָּלִין, וְזַרְעוֹ יִירַשׁ אָרֶץ:
יד. סוֹד יהוה לִירֵאָיו, וּבְרִיתוֹ לְהוֹדִיעָם:
טו. עֵינַי תָּמִיד אֶל־יהוה, כִּי הוּא־יוֹצִיא מֵרֶשֶׁת

Psalm – 25

In this Psalm one acknowledges his sin and begs to be taught the way to come close to Hashem.

1. A Psalm of David; To you, Hashem, I lift up my soul:

2. O my God, I trust in You; let me not be ashamed, let not my enemies triumph over me:

3. Also, let none who waits on You be ashamed; let those who transgress without cause be ashamed:

4. Make me know Your ways, Hashem; teach me Your paths:

5. Lead me in Your truth, and teach me; for You are the God of my salvation; for You I wait all the day:

6. Remember, Hashem, your compassion and Your loving kindness; for they have been here forever:

7. Remember not the sins of my youth, nor my transgressions; according to Your loving kindness remember me for Your goodness' sake, Hashem:

8. Good and upright is Hashem; therefore He instructs sinners in the way:

9. He guides the humble in judgment; and He teaches the humble his way:

10. All the paths of Hashem are loving kindness and truth to those who keep His covenant and His testimonies:

11. For Your name's sake, Hashem, pardon my iniquity; for it is great:

12. Who is the man who fears Hashem? Him shall He teach in the way that He should choose:

13. His soul shall abide in prosperity; and his seed shall inherit the earth:

14. The counsel of Hashem is with those who fear Him; and He will reveal to them His covenant:

15. My eyes are always toward Hashem; for He shall pluck my feet out of the net:

רַגְלָי: טז. פְּנֵה אֵלַי וְחָנֵּנִי, כִּי־יָחִיד וְעָנִי אָנִי:

יז. צָרוֹת לְבָבִי הִרְחִיבוּ, מִמְּצוּקוֹתַי הוֹצִיאֵנִי:

יח. רְאֵה עָנְיִי וַעֲמָלִי, וְשָׂא לְכָל־חַטֹּאותָי:

יט. רְאֵה־אוֹיְבַי כִּי־רָבּוּ, וְשִׂנְאַת חָמָס שְׂנֵאוּנִי:

כ. שָׁמְרָה נַפְשִׁי וְהַצִּילֵנִי, אַל־אֵבוֹשׁ כִּי־חָסִיתִי
בָךְ: כא. תֹּם־וָיֹשֶׁר יִצְּרוּנִי, כִּי קִוִּיתִיךָ: כב. פְּדֵה
אֱלֹהִים אֶת־יִשְׂרָאֵל, מִכֹּל צָרוֹתָיו:

תהלים – כז

In this Psalm we beg to be brought close to Hashem and plead that our
transgressions do not cause Hashem to conceal Himself from us.

א. לְדָוִד יהוה אוֹרִי וְיִשְׁעִי מִמִּי אִירָא, יהוה
מָעוֹז־חַיַּי, מִמִּי אֶפְחָד: ב. בִּקְרֹב עָלַי מְרֵעִים,
לֶאֱכֹל אֶת־בְּשָׂרִי, צָרַי וְאֹיְבַי לִי, הֵמָּה כָשְׁלוּ
וְנָפָלוּ: ג. אִם־תַּחֲנֶה עָלַי מַחֲנֶה, לֹא־יִירָא לִבִּי,
אִם־תָּקוּם עָלַי מִלְחָמָה, בְּזֹאת אֲנִי בוֹטֵחַ: ד. אַחַת
שָׁאַלְתִּי מֵאֵת־יהוה, אוֹתָהּ אֲבַקֵּשׁ, שִׁבְתִּי
בְּבֵית־יהוה כָּל־יְמֵי חַיַּי, לַחֲזוֹת בְּנֹעַם יהוה,
וּלְבַקֵּר בְּהֵיכָלוֹ: ה. כִּי יִצְפְּנֵנִי בְּסֻכֹּה בְּיוֹם רָעָה,
יַסְתִּרֵנִי בְּסֵתֶר אָהֳלוֹ, בְּצוּר יְרוֹמְמֵנִי: ו. וְעַתָּה

16. Turn to me, and be gracious to me; for I am desolate and afflicted:

17. The troubles of my heart are enlarged; O bring me out of my distresses:

18. Look upon my affliction and my pain; and forgive all my sins:

19. Consider my enemies; for they are many; and they hate me with a cruel hatred:

20. O keep my soul, and save me; let me not be ashamed; for I put my trust in You:

21. Let integrity and uprightness preserve me; for I wait on You:

22. Redeem Israel, O God, out of all his troubles:

Psalm – 27

In this Psalm we beg to be brought close to Hashem and plead that our transgressions do not cause Hashem to conceal Himself from us.

1. A Psalm of David; Hashem is my light and my salvation; Whom shall I fear? Hashem is the strength of my life; Of whom shall I be afraid:

2. When the wicked, my enemies and my adversaries, came upon me to eat up my flesh, they stumbled and fell:

3. Though a host should encamp against me, my heart shall not fear; though war should rise against me, even then I will be confident:

4. One thing have I desired of Hashem, I will constantly seek it; that I may dwell in the house of Hashem all the days of my life, to behold the beauty of Hashem, and to inquire in His Temple:

5. For in the time of trouble He shall hide me in His pavilion; under the cover of His tent shall He hide me; He shall set me up upon a rock:

6. And now shall my head be lifted up above my enemies

יָרוּם רֹאשִׁי עַל אֹיְבַי סְבִיבוֹתַי, וְאֶזְבְּחָה בְאָהֳלוֹ זִבְחֵי תְרוּעָה, אָשִׁירָה וַאֲזַמְּרָה לַיהוָה: ז. שְׁמַע־יהוה קוֹלִי אֶקְרָא, וְחָנֵּנִי וַעֲנֵנִי: ח. לְךָ אָמַר לִבִּי בַּקְּשׁוּ פָנָי, אֶת־פָּנֶיךָ יהוה אֲבַקֵּשׁ: ט. אַל־תַּסְתֵּר פָּנֶיךָ מִמֶּנִּי, אַל־תַּט־בְּאַף עַבְדֶּךָ, עֶזְרָתִי הָיִיתָ, אַל־תִּטְּשֵׁנִי וְאַל־תַּעַזְבֵנִי אֱלֹהֵי יִשְׁעִי: י. כִּי־אָבִי וְאִמִּי עֲזָבוּנִי, וַיהוָה יַאַסְפֵנִי: יא. הוֹרֵנִי יהוה דַּרְכֶּךָ, וּנְחֵנִי בְּאֹרַח מִישׁוֹר, לְמַעַן שׁוֹרְרָי: יב. אַל תִּתְּנֵנִי בְּנֶפֶשׁ צָרָי, כִּי קָמוּ־בִי עֵדֵי־שֶׁקֶר וִיפֵחַ חָמָס: יג. לוּלֵא הֶאֱמַנְתִּי, לִרְאוֹת בְּטוּב־יהוה בְּאֶרֶץ חַיִּים: יד. קַוֵּה אֶל־יהוה, חֲזַק וְיַאֲמֵץ לִבֶּךָ, וְקַוֵּה אֶל־יהוה:

תהלים – לב

David praises the one who recognizes his sin. He repents and acknowledges his guilt.

א. לְדָוִד מַשְׂכִּיל, אַשְׁרֵי נְשׂוּי־פֶּשַׁע כְּסוּי חֲטָאָה: ב. אַשְׁרֵי־אָדָם לֹא יַחְשֹׁב יהוה לוֹ עָוֹן, וְאֵין בְּרוּחוֹ רְמִיָּה: ג. כִּי־הֶחֱרַשְׁתִּי בָּלוּ עֲצָמָי, בְּשַׁאֲגָתִי כָּל־הַיּוֹם: ד. כִּי יוֹמָם וָלַיְלָה תִּכְבַּד

around me; therefore I will offer in His tent sacrifices of joy; I will sing, I will make music to Hashem:

7. Hear, Hashem, when I cry with my voice; be gracious to me, and answer me:

8. Of You my heart said, "Seek my face; Your face, Hashem, will I seek:"

9. Hide not Your face from me; put not Your servant away in anger; You have been my help; do not abandon me, nor forsake me, O God of my salvation:

10. For my father and my mother have forsaken me, but Hashem will take me up:

11. Teach me Your way, Hashem, and lead me on a level path, because of my enemies:

12. Do not give me up to the will of my enemies; for false witnesses have risen up against me, and they breathe out violence:

13. Were it not that I believe I should see the goodness of Hashem in the land of the living:

14. Wait on Hashem; be of good courage, and strengthen your heart; and wait on Hashem:

Psalm – 32

David praises the one who recognizes his sin. He repents and acknowledges his guilt.

1. A Psalm of David, A Maskil; Happy is he whose transgression is forgiven, whose sin is covered:

2. Happy is the man to whom Hashem does not impute iniquity, and in whose spirit there is no guile:

3. When I kept silence, my bones wasted away through my groaning all day long:

4. For day and night Your hand was heavy on me; my

עָלַי יָדֶךָ, נֶהְפַּךְ לְשַׁדִּי בְּחַרְבֹנֵי קַיִץ סֶלָה: ה. חַטָּאתִי אוֹדִיעֲךָ, וַעֲוֹנִי לֹא־כִסִּיתִי, אָמַרְתִּי אוֹדֶה עֲלֵי פְשָׁעַי לַיהוָה, וְאַתָּה נָשָׂאתָ עֲוֹן חַטָּאתִי סֶלָה: ו. עַל־זֹאת יִתְפַּלֵּל כָּל־חָסִיד אֵלֶיךָ לְעֵת מְצֹא, רַק לְשֵׁטֶף מַיִם רַבִּים אֵלָיו לֹא יַגִּיעוּ: ז. אַתָּה סֵתֶר לִי, מִצַּר תִּצְּרֵנִי, רָנֵּי פַלֵּט תְּסוֹבְבֵנִי סֶלָה: ח. אַשְׂכִּילְךָ וְאוֹרְךָ בְּדֶרֶךְ זוּ תֵלֵךְ, אִיעֲצָה עָלֶיךָ עֵינִי: ט. אַל־תִּהְיוּ כְּסוּס כְּפֶרֶד אֵין הָבִין, בְּמֶתֶג־וָרֶסֶן עֶדְיוֹ לִבְלוֹם, בַּל קְרֹב אֵלֶיךָ: י. רַבִּים מַכְאוֹבִים לָרָשָׁע, וְהַבּוֹטֵחַ בַּיהוָה חֶסֶד יְסוֹבְבֶנּוּ: יא. שִׂמְחוּ בַיהוָה וְגִילוּ צַדִּיקִים, וְהַרְנִינוּ כָּל־יִשְׁרֵי־לֵב:

תהלים – לח

David begs that he not be punished because of his sins. He realizes that he is not deserving of favors.

א. מִזְמוֹר לְדָוִד לְהַזְכִּיר: ב. יְהוָה אַל־בְּקֶצְפְּךָ תוֹכִיחֵנִי, וּבַחֲמָתְךָ תְיַסְּרֵנִי: ג. כִּי־חִצֶּיךָ נִחֲתוּ בִי, וַתִּנְחַת עָלַי יָדֶךָ: ד. אֵין־מְתֹם בִּבְשָׂרִי מִפְּנֵי

---

3. *To cause Hashem to remember the troubles that have befallen Israel.*

moisture is turned into the drought of summer; Selah:

5. I acknowledged my sin to You, and I did not hide my iniquity; I said, I will confess my transgressions to Hashem; and You forgave the iniquity of my sin; Selah:

6. For this[1] shall every one who is pious pray to You in a time when You may be found; then surely the floods of great waters shall not come near him:

7. You are my hiding place; You shall preserve me from trouble; You shall surround me with songs of deliverance; Selah:

8. I will instruct you and teach you in the way which you shall go; I will counsel you with my eye upon you:

9. Do not be like the horse, or like the mule, which have no understanding; whose mouth must be held in with bit and bridle,[2] lest they come near you:

10. Many are the sorrows of the wicked; but loving kindness shall surround him who trusts in Hashem:

11. Be glad in Hashem, and rejoice, you righteous; and shout for joy, all you who are upright in heart:

Psalm – 38

David begs that he not be punished because of his sins. He realizes that he is not deserving of favors.

1. A Psalm of David, to bring to remembrance:[3]

2. Hashem, rebuke me not in Your anger; nor chasten me in Your wrath:

3. For Your arrows stick fast in me, and Your hand presses me hard:

---

1. *One should pray that the flood waters of ones enemies should not destroy him.*

2. *A horse and mule must be restrained for their own good so they do not cause harm. So too we must realize that everything that befalls us is for our own good.*

זַעְמֶךָ, אֵין־שָׁלוֹם בַּעֲצָמַי מִפְּנֵי חַטָּאתִי: ה. כִּי
עֲוֹנֹתַי עָבְרוּ רֹאשִׁי, כְּמַשָּׂא כָבֵד יִכְבְּדוּ מִמֶּנִּי:
ו. הִבְאִישׁוּ נָמַקּוּ חַבּוּרֹתָי, מִפְּנֵי אִוַּלְתִּי:
ז. נַעֲוֵיתִי שַׁחֹתִי עַד־מְאֹד, כָּל־הַיּוֹם קֹדֵר
הִלָּכְתִּי: ח. כִּי־כְסָלַי מָלְאוּ נִקְלֶה, וְאֵין מְתֹם
בִּבְשָׂרִי: ט. נְפוּגֹתִי וְנִדְכֵּיתִי עַד־מְאֹד, שָׁאַגְתִּי
מִנַּהֲמַת לִבִּי: י. אֲדֹנָי נֶגְדְּךָ כָל־תַּאֲוָתִי, וְאַנְחָתִי
מִמְּךָ לֹא־נִסְתָּרָה: יא. לִבִּי סְחַרְחַר, עֲזָבַנִי כֹחִי,
וְאוֹר־עֵינַי גַּם־הֵם אֵין אִתִּי: יב. אֹהֲבַי וְרֵעַי
מִנֶּגֶד נִגְעִי יַעֲמֹדוּ, וּקְרוֹבַי מֵרָחֹק עָמָדוּ:
יג. וַיְנַקְשׁוּ מְבַקְשֵׁי נַפְשִׁי, וְדֹרְשֵׁי רָעָתִי דִּבְּרוּ
הַוּוֹת, וּמִרְמוֹת כָּל־הַיּוֹם יֶהְגּוּ: יד. וַאֲנִי כְחֵרֵשׁ
לֹא אֶשְׁמָע, וּכְאִלֵּם לֹא יִפְתַּח־פִּיו: טו. וָאֱהִי
כְּאִישׁ אֲשֶׁר לֹא־שֹׁמֵעַ, וְאֵין בְּפִיו תּוֹכָחוֹת:
טז. כִּי־לְךָ יְהֹוָה הוֹחָלְתִּי, אַתָּה תַעֲנֶה אֲדֹנָי
אֱלֹהָי: יז. כִּי־אָמַרְתִּי פֶּן־יִשְׂמְחוּ־לִי, בְּמוֹט רַגְלִי
עָלַי הִגְדִּילוּ: יח. כִּי־אֲנִי לְצֶלַע נָכוֹן, וּמַכְאוֹבִי
נֶגְדִּי תָמִיד: יט. כִּי־עֲוֹנִי אַגִּיד, אֶדְאַג מֵחַטָּאתִי:
כ. וְאֹיְבַי חַיִּים עָצֵמוּ, וְרַבּוּ שֹׂנְאַי שָׁקֶר:

4. There is no soundness in my flesh because of Your anger; nor is there any rest in my bones because of my sin:

5. For my iniquities have gone over my head; like a heavy burden they are too heavy for me:

6. My wounds grow foul and fester because of my foolishness:

7. I am troubled; I am bowed down greatly; I go mourning all the day long:

8. For my loins are filled with burning; and there is no soundness in my flesh:

9. I am feeble and crushed; I groan because of the tumult of my heart:

10. Hashem, all my desire is before You; and my sighing is not hidden from You:

11. My heart throbs, my strength fails me; as for the light of my eyes, it also is gone from me:

12. My lovers and my friends stand aloof from my plague; and my kinsmen stand far away:

13. Those who seek after my life lay snares for me; and those who seek my hurt speak mischievous things, and plot deceits all the day long:

14. But I am like a deaf man who does not hear; I am like a dumb man who does not open his mouth:

15. Thus I was like a man who does not hear, and in whose mouth there are no rebukes:

16. For in You, Hashem, I hope; You will answer, Hashem my God:

17. For I said, "Lest they should rejoice over me; when my foot slips, they magnify themselves against me:"

18. For I am ready to fall, and my pain is continually before me:

19. For I will declare my iniquity; I will be sorry for my sin:

20. But my living enemies are strong; and those who hate

כא. וּמְשַׁלְּמֵי רָעָה תַּחַת טוֹבָה, יִשְׂטְנוּנִי תַּחַת רָדְפִי־טוֹב: כב. אַל־תַּעַזְבֵנִי יְהֹוָה, אֱלֹהַי אַל־תִּרְחַק מִמֶּנִּי: כג. חוּשָׁה לְעֶזְרָתִי, אֲדֹנָי תְּשׁוּעָתִי:

תהלים – נא

This Psalm is an inspiration to all who sincerely desire to repent and who wish to beseech God for forgiveness.

א. לַמְנַצֵּחַ מִזְמוֹר לְדָוִד: ב. בְּבוֹא־אֵלָיו נָתָן הַנָּבִיא, כַּאֲשֶׁר־בָּא אֶל־בַּת־שָׁבַע: ג. חָנֵּנִי אֱלֹהִים כְּחַסְדֶּךָ, כְּרֹב רַחֲמֶיךָ מְחֵה פְשָׁעָי: ד. הֶרֶב כַּבְּסֵנִי מֵעֲוֹנִי, וּמֵחַטָּאתִי טַהֲרֵנִי: ה. כִּי־פְשָׁעַי אֲנִי אֵדָע, וְחַטָּאתִי נֶגְדִּי תָמִיד: ו. לְךָ לְבַדְּךָ חָטָאתִי, וְהָרַע בְּעֵינֶיךָ עָשִׂיתִי, לְמַעַן תִּצְדַּק בְּדָבְרֶךָ, תִּזְכֶּה בְשָׁפְטֶךָ: ז. הֵן־בְּעָווֹן חוֹלָלְתִּי, וּבְחֵטְא יֶחֱמַתְנִי אִמִּי: ח. הֵן־אֱמֶת חָפַצְתָּ בַטֻּחוֹת, וּבְסָתֻם חָכְמָה תוֹדִיעֵנִי: ט. תְּחַטְּאֵנִי בְאֵזוֹב וְאֶטְהָר, תְּכַבְּסֵנִי וּמִשֶּׁלֶג

---

person. They are considered to be the seat of intellect – see Psalms 7:10, 16:7; Job 38:36. The intent here is to present truth with a deep inner conviction.

me wrongfully are many:

21. Those who repay evil for good are my adversaries because I pursue good deeds.

22. Do not forsake me, Hashem! O my God, do not be far from me:

23. Make haste to help me, Hashem my salvation:

Psalm – 51

This Psalm is an inspiration to all who sincerely desire to repent and who wish to beseech God for forgiveness.

1. To the Chief Musician, a Psalm of David.

2. When Nathan the prophet came to him, after he had come to Bath Sheva.

3. Be gracious unto me, O God, according to Your kindness, obliterate my transgressions according to Your abundant mercies.

4. Thoroughly cleanse me from my iniquity, and purify me from my sin.

5. For I fully acknowledge my transgressions, and my sin is ever before me.

6. Against You alone have I sinned and done that which is evil in Your eyes, so that You would be justified when You speak and equitable when You judge.

7. Behold, I was created in inquity, and in sin did my mother conceive me.

8. Behold, You desire truth from deep within me[1], and in my innermost heart you informed me of wisdom.

9. Purge me of sin with hyssop and I shall be pure, cleanse me and I shall be whiter than snow.

---

1. *The word 'vatuchos' actually means kidneys which are deeply concealed within the*

אַלְבִּין: י. תַּשְׁמִיעֵנִי שָׂשׂוֹן וְשִׂמְחָה, תָּגֵלְנָה
עֲצָמוֹת דִּכִּיתָ: יא. הַסְתֵּר פָּנֶיךָ מֵחֲטָאָי, וְכָל־
עֲוֹנֹתַי מְחֵה: יב. לֵב טָהוֹר בְּרָא־לִי אֱלֹהִים,
וְרוּחַ נָכוֹן חַדֵּשׁ בְּקִרְבִּי: יג. אַל־תַּשְׁלִיכֵנִי
מִלְּפָנֶיךָ, וְרוּחַ קָדְשְׁךָ אַל־תִּקַּח מִמֶּנִּי:
יד. הָשִׁיבָה לִּי שְׂשׂוֹן יִשְׁעֶךָ, וְרוּחַ נְדִיבָה
תִסְמְכֵנִי: טו. אֲלַמְּדָה פֹשְׁעִים דְּרָכֶיךָ, וְחַטָּאִים
אֵלֶיךָ יָשׁוּבוּ: טז. הַצִּילֵנִי מִדָּמִים, אֱלֹהִים אֱלֹהֵי
תְּשׁוּעָתִי, תְּרַנֵּן לְשׁוֹנִי צִדְקָתֶךָ: יז. אֲדֹנָי שְׂפָתַי
תִּפְתָּח, וּפִי יַגִּיד תְּהִלָּתֶךָ: יח. כִּי לֹא־תַחְפֹּץ
זֶבַח וְאֶתֵּנָה, עוֹלָה לֹא תִרְצֶה: יט. זִבְחֵי אֱלֹהִים
רוּחַ נִשְׁבָּרָה, לֵב־נִשְׁבָּר וְנִדְכֶּה אֱלֹהִים לֹא
תִבְזֶה: כ. הֵיטִיבָה בִרְצוֹנְךָ אֶת־צִיּוֹן, תִּבְנֶה
חוֹמוֹת יְרוּשָׁלָיִם: כא. אָז תַּחְפֹּץ זִבְחֵי־צֶדֶק
עוֹלָה וְכָלִיל, אָז יַעֲלוּ עַל־מִזְבַּחֲךָ פָרִים:

תהלים - פה

We beg Hashem to accept our repentance and return to us. Unity
between us and Hashem will cause the land to give forth its produce.

א. לַמְנַצֵּחַ לִבְנֵי קֹרַח, מִזְמוֹר: ב. רָצִיתָ יְהֹוָה

10. Make me hear joy and gladness, then the bones which you crushed will rejoice.

11. Hide Your face from my sins, and eradicate all my inquities.

12. Create for me a pure heart, O God, and renew within me a virtuous spirit.

13. Cast me not away from Your Presence, and do not take from me Your Holy Spirit.

14. Restore to me the joy of Your salvation and support me with a munificent spirit.

15. [Then] I will teach transgressors Your ways, and sinners shall return unto You.

16. Save me from death, O God, God of my salvation, then shall my tongue sing joyously of Your righteousness.

17. My Lord, open my lips, and my mouth will declare your praise.

18. For You have no desire of a sacrifice, else I would give it, [and] You do not want a burnt-offering.

19. [Of all] the sacrifices to God, [the most pleasing] is a broken spirit; a heart broken and crushed, O God, You will not despise.

20. Do good unto Zion in Your favor, [and] build the walls of Jerusalem.

21. Then You will desire the sacrifices of righteousness, burnt-offering and whole-offering; then they will offer bullocks upon Your altar.

Psalm – 85

We beg Hashem to accept our repentance and return to us. Unity between us and Hashem will cause the land to give forth its produce.

1. To the chief Musician, A Psalm for the sons of Korah:

אַרְצֶךָ, שַׁבְתָּ שְׁבִית יַעֲקֹב: ג. נָשָׂאתָ עֲוֹן עַמֶּךָ, כִּסִּיתָ כָל חַטָּאתָם סֶלָה: ד. אָסַפְתָּ כָל עֶבְרָתֶךָ, הֱשִׁיבוֹתָ מֵחֲרוֹן אַפֶּךָ: ה. שׁוּבֵנוּ אֱלֹהֵי יִשְׁעֵנוּ, וְהָפֵר כַּעַסְךָ עִמָּנוּ: ו. הַלְעוֹלָם תֶּאֱנַף בָּנוּ, תִּמְשֹׁךְ אַפְּךָ לְדֹר וָדֹר: ז. הֲלֹא אַתָּה תָּשׁוּב תְּחַיֵּינוּ, וְעַמְּךָ יִשְׂמְחוּ בָךְ: ח. הַרְאֵנוּ יְהוָה חַסְדֶּךָ, וְיֶשְׁעֲךָ תִּתֶּן לָנוּ: ט. אֶשְׁמְעָה מַה יְדַבֵּר הָאֵל יְהוָה, כִּי יְדַבֵּר שָׁלוֹם אֶל עַמּוֹ וְאֶל חֲסִידָיו, וְאַל יָשׁוּבוּ לְכִסְלָה: י. אַךְ קָרוֹב לִירֵאָיו יִשְׁעוֹ, לִשְׁכֹּן כָּבוֹד בְּאַרְצֵנוּ: יא. חֶסֶד וֶאֱמֶת נִפְגָּשׁוּ, צֶדֶק וְשָׁלוֹם נָשָׁקוּ: יב. אֱמֶת מֵאֶרֶץ תִּצְמָח, וְצֶדֶק מִשָּׁמַיִם נִשְׁקָף: יג. גַּם יְהוָה יִתֵּן הַטּוֹב, וְאַרְצֵנוּ תִּתֵּן יְבוּלָהּ: יד. צֶדֶק לְפָנָיו יְהַלֵּךְ, וְיָשֵׂם לְדֶרֶךְ פְּעָמָיו:

תהלים - צ

Hashems power in this world is unlimited. It is incumbent on man to repent and be worthy of Divine favor.

א. תְּפִלָּה לְמֹשֶׁה אִישׁ-הָאֱלֹהִים, אֲדֹנָי מָעוֹן

2. Hashem, You have been favorable to Your land; You have brought back the captivity of Jacob:

3. You have forgiven the iniquity of Your people, You have pardoned all their sin; Selah:

4. You have withdrawn all Your wrath; You have turned from the fierceness of Your anger:

5. Restore us, O God of our salvation, and cease Your anger toward us:

6. Will You be angry with us for ever? Will You draw out Your anger to all generations:

7. Will You not revive us again, that Your people may rejoice in you:

8. Show us Your loving kindness, O Hashem, and grant us Your salvation:

9. I will hear what God, Hashem, will speak; for He will speak peace to His people, and to His pious ones; but let them not turn back to folly:

10. Surely His salvation is near to those who fear Him; that glory may dwell in our land:

11. Loving kindness and truth meet together; righteousness and peace kiss each other:

12. Truth shall spring from the earth; and righteousness shall look down from heaven:

13. Also, Hashem shall give that which is good; and our land shall yield her produce:

14. Righteousness shall go before Him; and walk in the way of His steps:

Psalm – 90

Hashems power in this world is unlimited. It is incumbent on man to repent and be worthy of Divine favor.

1. A Prayer of Moses the man of God; Lord, You have

אַתָּה הָיִיתָ לָּנוּ בְּדֹר וָדֹר: ב. בְּטֶרֶם הָרִים יֻלָּדוּ,
וַתְּחוֹלֵל אֶרֶץ וְתֵבֵל, וּמֵעוֹלָם עַד־עוֹלָם אַתָּה
אֵל: ג. תָּשֵׁב אֱנוֹשׁ עַד־דַּכָּא, וַתֹּאמֶר שׁוּבוּ בְנֵי
אָדָם: ד. כִּי אֶלֶף שָׁנִים בְּעֵינֶיךָ כְּיוֹם אֶתְמוֹל
כִּי יַעֲבֹר, וְאַשְׁמוּרָה בַלָּיְלָה: ה. זְרַמְתָּם שֵׁנָה
יִהְיוּ, בַּבֹּקֶר כֶּחָצִיר יַחֲלֹף: ו. בַּבֹּקֶר יָצִיץ וְחָלָף,
לָעֶרֶב יְמוֹלֵל וְיָבֵשׁ: ז. כִּי־כָלִינוּ בְאַפֶּךָ,
וּבַחֲמָתְךָ נִבְהָלְנוּ: ח. שַׁתָּ עֲוֹנֹתֵינוּ לְנֶגְדֶּךָ,
עֲלֻמֵנוּ לִמְאוֹר פָּנֶיךָ: ט. כִּי כָל־יָמֵינוּ פָּנוּ
בְעֶבְרָתֶךָ, כִּלִּינוּ שָׁנֵינוּ כְמוֹ־הֶגֶה: י. יְמֵי־
שְׁנוֹתֵינוּ בָהֶם שִׁבְעִים שָׁנָה, וְאִם בִּגְבוּרֹת
שְׁמוֹנִים שָׁנָה, וְרָהְבָּם עָמָל וָאָוֶן, כִּי־גָז חִישׁ
וַנָּעֻפָה: יא. מִי־יוֹדֵעַ עֹז אַפֶּךָ, וּכְיִרְאָתְךָ
עֶבְרָתֶךָ: יב. לִמְנוֹת יָמֵינוּ כֵּן הוֹדַע, וְנָבִא לְבַב
חָכְמָה: יג. שׁוּבָה יְהוָה עַד־מָתָי, וְהִנָּחֵם עַל־
עֲבָדֶיךָ: יד. שַׂבְּעֵנוּ בַבֹּקֶר חַסְדֶּךָ, וּנְרַנְּנָה
וְנִשְׂמְחָה בְּכָל־יָמֵינוּ: טו. שַׂמְּחֵנוּ כִּימוֹת עִנִּיתָנוּ,
שְׁנוֹת רָאִינוּ רָעָה: טז. יֵרָאֶה אֶל־עֲבָדֶיךָ פָעֳלֶךָ,
וַהֲדָרְךָ עַל־בְּנֵיהֶם: יז. וִיהִי נֹעַם אֲדֹנָי אֱלֹהֵינוּ

been our dwelling place in all generations:

2. Before the mountains were brought forth, before You had formed the earth and the world, forever and forever, You are God:

3. You turn man back to dust; and say, "Turn back, O children of men:"

4. For a thousand years in Your eyes are but like yesterday that has past, and like a watch in the night:

5. You sweep them away; they are like sleepers; they are like short lived grass in the morning:

6. In the morning it flourishes, and fades; by evening it is withered and dry:

7. For we are consumed by Your anger, and by Your wrath are we terrified:

8. You have set our iniquities before You, our secret sins in the light of Your countenance:

9. For all our days pass away in Your wrath; we spend our years like a tale that is told:

10. The days of our years are seventy; or if, because of strength, they are eighty years, yet their pride is but trouble and wretchedness; for it is soon cut off, and we fly away:

11. Who knows the power of Your anger? According to Your fear, so is Your wrath:

12. So teach us to count our days, that we may get a heart of wisdom:

13. Return, Hashem! How long? And relent concerning Your servants:

14. O satisfy us in the morning with Your loving kindness; that we may rejoice and be glad all our days:

15. Make us glad as many days as You have afflicted us, and as many years as we have seen evil:

16. Let Your work be visible to Your servants, and Your glory to their children:

17. And let the beauty of Hashem our God be upon us;

עָלֵינוּ, וּמַעֲשֵׂה יָדֵינוּ כּוֹנְנָה עָלֵינוּ, וּמַעֲשֵׂה
יָדֵינוּ כּוֹנְנֵהוּ:

תהלים – צה

After proclaiming that Hashem is master of everything the Psalmist
directs man not to follow the path of our ancestors who sinned in the
desert.

א. לְכוּ נְרַנְּנָה לַיהוָה, נָרִיעָה לְצוּר יִשְׁעֵנוּ:
ב. נְקַדְּמָה פָנָיו בְּתוֹדָה, בִּזְמִרוֹת נָרִיעַ לוֹ: ג. כִּי
אֵל גָּדוֹל יְהוָה, וּמֶלֶךְ גָּדוֹל עַל־כָּל־אֱלֹהִים:
ד. אֲשֶׁר בְּיָדוֹ מֶחְקְרֵי־אָרֶץ, וְתוֹעֲפוֹת הָרִים לוֹ:
ה. אֲשֶׁר־לוֹ הַיָּם וְהוּא עָשָׂהוּ, וְיַבֶּשֶׁת יָדָיו יָצָרוּ:
ו. בֹּאוּ נִשְׁתַּחֲוֶה וְנִכְרָעָה, נִבְרְכָה לִפְנֵי־יְהוָה
עֹשֵׂנוּ: ז. כִּי הוּא אֱלֹהֵינוּ, וַאֲנַחְנוּ עַם מַרְעִיתוֹ
וְצֹאן יָדוֹ, הַיּוֹם אִם־בְּקֹלוֹ תִשְׁמָעוּ: ח. אַל תַּקְשׁוּ
לְבַבְכֶם כִּמְרִיבָה, כְּיוֹם מַסָּה בַּמִּדְבָּר: ט. אֲשֶׁר
נִסּוּנִי אֲבוֹתֵיכֶם בְּחָנוּנִי, גַּם־רָאוּ פָעֳלִי:
י. אַרְבָּעִים שָׁנָה אָקוּט בְּדוֹר, וָאֹמַר עַם תֹּעֵי
לֵבָב הֵם, וְהֵם לֹא־יָדְעוּ דְרָכָי: יא. אֲשֶׁר
נִשְׁבַּעְתִּי בְאַפִּי, אִם־יְבֹאוּן אֶל־מְנוּחָתִי:

and establish the work of our hands upon us; O prosper it, the work of our hands:

Psalm – 95

After proclaiming that Hashem is master of everything the Psalmist directs man not to follow the path of our ancestors who sinned in the desert.

1. O come, let us sing to Hashem; let us make a joyful noise to the rock of our salvation:

2. Let us come before His presence with thanksgiving, and make a joyful noise to Him with psalms:

3. For Hashem is a great God, and a great King above all gods:

4. In His hand are the deep places of the earth; the heights of the mountains are also His:

5. The sea is His, and He made it; and His hands formed the dry land:

6. O come, let us worship and bow down; let us kneel before Hashem our Maker:

7. For He is our God; and we are the people of His pasture, and the sheep of His hand; Even today, if you will only listen to His voice:

8. Do not harden your hearts, like you did at Meribah, and like you did in the day of Massah in the wilderness:

9. When your fathers tempted Me, and tested Me, even though they had seen My deeds:

10. For forty years I loathed that generation, and said, "They are a people who err in their heart, and they do not know my ways":

11. Therefore I swore in My wrath that they should not enter into My rest:

תהלים – קו

This Psalm portrays the periods in our history when we were forsaken because of our sins and subsequently saved when we repented.

א. הַלְלוּיָהּ, הוֹדוּ לַיהוָה כִּי־טוֹב, כִּי לְעוֹלָם חַסְדּוֹ: ב. מִי יְמַלֵּל גְּבוּרוֹת יְהוָה, יַשְׁמִיעַ כָּל־תְּהִלָּתוֹ: ג. אַשְׁרֵי שֹׁמְרֵי מִשְׁפָּט, עֹשֵׂה צְדָקָה בְכָל־עֵת: ד. זָכְרֵנִי יְהוָה בִּרְצוֹן עַמֶּךָ, פָּקְדֵנִי בִּישׁוּעָתֶךָ: ה. לִרְאוֹת בְּטוֹבַת בְּחִירֶיךָ, לִשְׂמֹחַ בְּשִׂמְחַת גּוֹיֶךָ, לְהִתְהַלֵּל עִם־נַחֲלָתֶךָ: ו. חָטָאנוּ עִם־אֲבוֹתֵינוּ, הֶעֱוִינוּ הִרְשָׁעְנוּ: ז. אֲבוֹתֵינוּ בְמִצְרַיִם לֹא־הִשְׂכִּילוּ נִפְלְאוֹתֶיךָ, לֹא זָכְרוּ אֶת־רֹב חֲסָדֶיךָ, וַיַּמְרוּ עַל־יָם בְּיַם־סוּף: ח. וַיּוֹשִׁיעֵם לְמַעַן שְׁמוֹ, לְהוֹדִיעַ אֶת־גְּבוּרָתוֹ: ט. וַיִּגְעַר בְּיַם־סוּף וַיֶּחֱרָב, וַיּוֹלִיכֵם בַּתְּהֹמוֹת כַּמִּדְבָּר: י. וַיּוֹשִׁיעֵם מִיַּד שׂוֹנֵא, וַיִּגְאָלֵם מִיַּד אוֹיֵב: יא. וַיְכַסּוּ־מַיִם צָרֵיהֶם, אֶחָד מֵהֶם לֹא נוֹתָר: יב. וַיַּאֲמִינוּ בִדְבָרָיו, יָשִׁירוּ תְּהִלָּתוֹ: יג. מִהֲרוּ שָׁכְחוּ מַעֲשָׂיו, לֹא־חִכּוּ לַעֲצָתוֹ: יד. וַיִּתְאַוּוּ תַאֲוָה בַּמִּדְבָּר, וַיְנַסּוּ־אֵל בִּישִׁימוֹן:

---

1. The red sea was split by a strong wind ; here this wind is compared to the anger and rebuke of Hashem.

Psalm – 106

This Psalm portrays the periods in our history when we were forsaken because of our sins and subsequently saved when we repented.

1. Halleluyah! O give thanks to Hashem; for He is good; for His loving kindness endures forever:

2. Who can utter the mighty acts of Hashem? Who can declare all His praise:

3. Happy are those who maintain justice, and he who does righteousness at all times:

4. Remember me, Hashem, when You show favor to Your people; O visit me with Your salvation:

5. That I may see the good of Your chosen, that I may rejoice in the gladness of Your nation, that I may glory with Your inheritance:

6. We have sinned with our fathers, we have committed iniquity, we have done wickedly:

7. Our fathers, when they were in Egypt, did not understand Your wonders; they did not remember the multitude of Your deeds of loving kindness; and they rebelled against You at the sea, the Red Sea:

8. But He saved them for His name's sake, that He might make known his mighty power:

9. And He rebuked the Red Sea[1], and it was dried up; and He led them through the depths, as through the desert:

10. And He saved them from the hand of him who hated them, and redeemed them from the hand of the enemy:

11. And the waters covered their enemies; there was not one of them left:

12. Then they believed His words; they sang His praise:

13. They soon forgot His works; they did not wait for His counsel:

14. They had wanton cravings in the wilderness, and put God to the test in the desert:

טו. וַיִּתֵּן לָהֶם שֶׁאֱלָתָם, וַיְשַׁלַּח רָזוֹן בְּנַפְשָׁם:

טז. וַיְקַנְאוּ לְמֹשֶׁה בַּמַּחֲנֶה, לְאַהֲרֹן קְדוֹשׁ יְהוָה:

יז. תִּפְתַּח־אֶרֶץ וַתִּבְלַע דָּתָן, וַתְּכַס עַל־עֲדַת אֲבִירָם:

יח. וַתִּבְעַר־אֵשׁ בַּעֲדָתָם, לֶהָבָה תְּלַהֵט רְשָׁעִים:

יט. יַעֲשׂוּ־עֵגֶל בְּחֹרֵב, וַיִּשְׁתַּחֲווּ לְמַסֵּכָה:

כ. וַיָּמִירוּ אֶת־כְּבוֹדָם, בְּתַבְנִית שׁוֹר אֹכֵל עֵשֶׂב:

כא. שָׁכְחוּ אֵל מוֹשִׁיעָם, עֹשֶׂה גְדֹלוֹת בְּמִצְרָיִם:

כב. נִפְלָאוֹת בְּאֶרֶץ חָם, נוֹרָאוֹת עַל־יַם־סוּף:

כג. וַיֹּאמֶר לְהַשְׁמִידָם, לוּלֵי מֹשֶׁה בְחִירוֹ עָמַד בַּפֶּרֶץ לְפָנָיו, לְהָשִׁיב חֲמָתוֹ מֵהַשְׁחִית:

כד. וַיִּמְאֲסוּ בְּאֶרֶץ חֶמְדָּה, לֹא הֶאֱמִינוּ לִדְבָרוֹ:

כה. וַיֵּרָגְנוּ בְאָהֳלֵיהֶם, לֹא שָׁמְעוּ בְּקוֹל יְהוָה:

כו. וַיִּשָּׂא יָדוֹ לָהֶם, לְהַפִּיל אוֹתָם בַּמִּדְבָּר:

כז. וּלְהַפִּיל זַרְעָם בַּגּוֹיִם, וּלְזָרוֹתָם בָּאֲרָצוֹת:

כח. וַיִּצָּמְדוּ לְבַעַל פְּעוֹר, וַיֹּאכְלוּ זִבְחֵי מֵתִים:

כט. וַיַּכְעִיסוּ בְּמַעַלְלֵיהֶם,

---

4. *Referring to the Golden Calf made at Sinai.*

5. *They exchanged Hashem for the Calf.*

6. *This refers to the spies who returned from Eretz Yisroel with a bad report about the land.*

7. *At the end of the forty years in the desert a large portion of the Jewish nation was tempted to idolatry.*

15. And He gave them what they asked; but sent leanness into their soul:

16. And they envied Moses[2] in the camp, and Aaron the holy one of Hashem:

17. The earth opened and swallowed up Dathan, and covered the company of Abiram:[3]

18. And a fire was kindled in their company; the flame burned up the wicked:

19. They made a calf in Horeb,[4] and worshipped the molten image:

20. Thus they changed their glory[5] for the likeness of an ox that eats grass:

21. They forgot God who had saved them, Who had done great things in Egypt:

22. Wondrous works in the land of Ham, and awesome things by the Red Sea:

23. Therefore He said that He would destroy them, had not Moses, His chosen one, stood before Him in the breach, to turn away His wrath, lest He should destroy them:

24. And they despised the pleasant land,[6] they did not believe His word:

25. And they murmured in their tents, and did not listen to the voice of Hashem:

26. And He lifted up his hand against them, to make them fall in the wilderness:

27. And to make their seed fall among the nations, and to scatter them in the lands:

28. And they joined themselves to Baal-Peor[7], and ate the sacrifices of the dead:

29. Thus they provoked Him to anger with their wrongdoings; and the plague broke out upon them:

---

2. *This refers to the argument of Korach and his congregation when they complained that Moshe took for himself the leadership of Klal Yisroel.*

3. *The earth swallowed Korach's congregation after his rebellion.*

וַתִּפְרָץ־בָּם מַגֵּפָה: ל. וַיַּעֲמֹד פִּינְחָס וַיְפַלֵּל,
וַתֵּעָצַר הַמַּגֵּפָה: לא. וַתֵּחָשֶׁב לוֹ לִצְדָקָה, לְדֹר
וָדֹר עַד־עוֹלָם: לב. וַיַּקְצִיפוּ עַל־מֵי מְרִיבָה,
וַיֵּרַע לְמֹשֶׁה בַּעֲבוּרָם: לג. כִּי־הִמְרוּ אֶת־רוּחוֹ,
וַיְבַטֵּא בִּשְׂפָתָיו: לד. לֹא־הִשְׁמִידוּ אֶת־הָעַמִּים,
אֲשֶׁר אָמַר יְהֹוָה לָהֶם: לה. וַיִּתְעָרְבוּ בַגּוֹיִם,
וַיִּלְמְדוּ מַעֲשֵׂיהֶם: לו. וַיַּעַבְדוּ אֶת־עֲצַבֵּיהֶם,
וַיִּהְיוּ לָהֶם לְמוֹקֵשׁ: לז. וַיִּזְבְּחוּ אֶת־בְּנֵיהֶם וְאֶת־
בְּנוֹתֵיהֶם לַשֵּׁדִים: לח. וַיִּשְׁפְּכוּ דָם נָקִי, דַּם־
בְּנֵיהֶם וּבְנוֹתֵיהֶם אֲשֶׁר זִבְּחוּ לַעֲצַבֵּי כְנַעַן,
וַתֶּחֱנַף הָאָרֶץ בַּדָּמִים: לט. וַיִּטְמְאוּ בְמַעֲשֵׂיהֶם,
וַיִּזְנוּ בְּמַעַלְלֵיהֶם: מ. וַיִּחַר־אַף יְהֹוָה בְּעַמּוֹ,
וַיְתָעֵב אֶת־נַחֲלָתוֹ: מא. וַיִּתְּנֵם בְּיַד־גּוֹיִם,
וַיִּמְשְׁלוּ בָהֶם שֹׂנְאֵיהֶם: מב. וַיִּלְחָצוּם אוֹיְבֵיהֶם,
וַיִּכָּנְעוּ תַּחַת יָדָם: מג. פְּעָמִים רַבּוֹת יַצִּילֵם,
וְהֵמָּה יַמְרוּ בַעֲצָתָם, וַיָּמֹכּוּ בַּעֲוֹנָם: מד. וַיַּרְא
בַּצַּר לָהֶם, בְּשָׁמְעוֹ אֶת־רִנָּתָם: מה. וַיִּזְכֹּר לָהֶם

---

9. Because of this action he was rewarded with Kehunah (Priesthood) for himself and his descendants.

10. The Jewish people complained for water at Meribah and at that time Moshe was punished.

11. After they entered the land of Israel they did not destroy the idolatrous nations as they had been commanded.

30. Then stood up Phinehas,[8] and executed judgment; and so the plague was stayed:

31. And that was counted to him for righteousness[9] to all generations for evermore:

32. And they angered Him at the waters of Meribah,[10] so that it went ill with Moses because of them:

33. Because they angered His spirit, so that He spoke rashly with His lips:

34. They did not destroy the nations, concerning whom Hashem commanded them:[11]

35. They mingled among the nations, and learned to do what they did:

36. And they served their idols; which became a snare to them:

37. And they sacrificed their sons and their daughters to idols:

38. And shed innocent blood, the blood of their sons and of their daughters, whom they sacrificed to the idols of Canaan; and the land was polluted with blood:

39. Thus were they defiled with their own works, and went astray in their doings:

40. And the wrath of Hashem was kindled against His people, and He loathed His own heritage:

41. And He gave them into the hand of the nations; and those who hated them ruled over them:

42. And their enemies oppressed them, and they were brought into subjection under their hand:

43. Many times He saved them; but they were rebellious in their counsel, and were brought low for their iniquity:

44. Nevertheless, when He heard their cry, He regarded their affliction:

45. And He remembered for them His covenant, and

---

8. *Pinchas when he zealously stopped the nation from desecrating Hashems name.*

בְּרִיתוֹ, וַיִּנָּחֵם כְּרֹב חֲסָדָיו: מו. וַיִּתֵּן אוֹתָם
לְרַחֲמִים, לִפְנֵי כָּל־שׁוֹבֵיהֶם: מז. הוֹשִׁיעֵנוּ יְהוָה
אֱלֹהֵינוּ וְקַבְּצֵנוּ מִן־הַגּוֹיִם, לְהֹדוֹת לְשֵׁם
קָדְשֶׁךָ, לְהִשְׁתַּבֵּחַ בִּתְהִלָּתֶךָ: מח. בָּרוּךְ־יְהוָה
אֱלֹהֵי יִשְׂרָאֵל, מִן־הָעוֹלָם וְעַד הָעוֹלָם, וְאָמַר
כָּל־הָעָם אָמֵן הַלְלוּיָהּ:

תהלים – קל

This Psalm describes one who calls out to Hashem from the depths of sin, begging for forgiveness.

א. שִׁיר הַמַּעֲלוֹת, מִמַּעֲמַקִּים קְרָאתִיךָ יְהוָה:
ב. אֲדֹנָי שִׁמְעָה בְקוֹלִי, תִּהְיֶינָה אָזְנֶיךָ קַשֻּׁבוֹת
לְקוֹל תַּחֲנוּנָי: ג. אִם־עֲוֹנוֹת תִּשְׁמָר־יָהּ, אֲדֹנָי
מִי יַעֲמֹד: ד. כִּי־עִמְּךָ הַסְּלִיחָה, לְמַעַן תִּוָּרֵא:
ה. קִוִּיתִי יְהוָה קִוְּתָה נַפְשִׁי, וְלִדְבָרוֹ הוֹחָלְתִּי:
ו. נַפְשִׁי לַאדֹנָי מִשֹּׁמְרִים לַבֹּקֶר, שֹׁמְרִים לַבֹּקֶר:
ז. יַחֵל יִשְׂרָאֵל אֶל־יְהוָה, כִּי־עִם־יְהוָה הַחֶסֶד,
וְהַרְבֵּה עִמּוֹ פְדוּת: ח. וְהוּא יִפְדֶּה אֶת־יִשְׂרָאֵל,
מִכֹּל עֲוֹנוֹתָיו:

relented according to the abundance of His loving kindness:

46. And He caused them to be pitied by all those who held them captive:

47. Save us, Hashem our God, and gather us from among the nations, that we may give thanks to Your holy name, and to triumph in Your praise:

48. Blessed be Hashem God of Israel forever and ever; and let all the people say, Amen; Halleluyah:

Psalm – 130

This Psalm describes one who calls out to Hashem from the depths of sin, begging for forgiveness.

1. A Song of Ascents; Out of the depths have I cry to You, Hashem:

2. Lord, hear My voice; let Your ears be attentive to the voice of My supplications:

3. If You, O Lord, should mark iniquities, Lord, who could stand:

4. But there is forgiveness with You, that You may be feared:

5. I wait for Hashem, my soul waits, and in His word I hope:

6. My soul waits for Lord more than those who watch for the morning watch for the morning:

7. Let Israel hope in Hashem; for with Hashem there is loving kindness, and with Him is bountiful redemption:

8. And He shall redeem Israel from all his iniquities:

תהלים - קלט

*This Psalm is a declaration that all of man's thoughts are known to
Hashem and He is aware of the sincerity of all his actions.*

א. לַמְנַצֵּחַ לְדָוִד מִזְמוֹר, יְהֹוָה חֲקַרְתַּנִי וַתֵּדָע:
ב. אַתָּה יָדַעְתָּ שִׁבְתִּי וְקוּמִי, בַּנְתָּה לְרֵעִי
מֵרָחוֹק: ג. אָרְחִי וְרִבְעִי זֵרִיתָ, וְכָל־דְּרָכַי
הִסְכַּנְתָּה: ד. כִּי אֵין מִלָּה בִּלְשׁוֹנִי, הֵן יְהֹוָה
יָדַעְתָּ כֻלָּהּ: ה. אָחוֹר וָקֶדֶם צַרְתָּנִי, וַתָּשֶׁת עָלַי
כַּפֶּכָה: ו. פְּלִיאָה דַעַת מִמֶּנִּי נִשְׂגְּבָה, לֹא־אוּכַל
לָהּ: ז. אָנָה אֵלֵךְ מֵרוּחֶךָ, וְאָנָה מִפָּנֶיךָ אֶבְרָח:
ח. אִם־אֶסַּק שָׁמַיִם שָׁם אָתָּה, וְאַצִּיעָה שְּׁאוֹל
הִנֶּךָּ: ט. אֶשָּׂא כַנְפֵי־שָׁחַר, אֶשְׁכְּנָה בְּאַחֲרִית
יָם: י. גַּם־שָׁם יָדְךָ תַנְחֵנִי, וְתֹאחֲזֵנִי יְמִינֶךָ:
יא. וָאֹמַר אַךְ־חֹשֶׁךְ יְשׁוּפֵנִי, וְלַיְלָה אוֹר בַּעֲדֵנִי:
יב. גַּם־חֹשֶׁךְ לֹא־יַחְשִׁיךְ מִמֶּךָ, וְלַיְלָה כַּיּוֹם
יָאִיר, כַּחֲשֵׁיכָה כָּאוֹרָה: יג. כִּי־אַתָּה קָנִיתָ
כִלְיֹתָי, תְּסֻכֵּנִי בְּבֶטֶן אִמִּי: יד. אוֹדְךָ עַל כִּי
נוֹרָאוֹת נִפְלֵיתִי, נִפְלָאִים מַעֲשֶׂיךָ, וְנַפְשִׁי
יֹדַעַת מְאֹד: טו. לֹא־נִכְחַד עָצְמִי מִמֶּךָ, אֲשֶׁר־
עֻשֵּׂיתִי בַסֵּתֶר, רֻקַּמְתִּי בְּתַחְתִּיּוֹת אָרֶץ:

Psalm – 139

This Psalm is a declaration that all of man's thoughts are known to Hashem and He is aware of the sincerity of all his actions.

1. To the chief Musician, A Psalm of David; Hashem, You have searched me, and known me:

2. You know when I sit down and when I rise up, You understand my thoughts from far away:

3. You have measured my going and my lying down, and You are acquainted with all my ways:

4. For before a word is in my tongue, behold, Hashem, you know it all:

5. You have created my front and back, and laid Your hand upon me:

6. Such knowledge is too wonderful for me; it is high, I cannot attain it:

7. Where shall I go from Your spirit? Where shall I flee from Your presence:

8. If I ascend up to heaven, You are there! If I make my bed in the grave, behold, You are there:

9. If I take the wings of the morning, and dwell in the uttermost parts of the sea:

10. Even there shall Your hand lead me, and Your right hand shall hold me:

11. If I say, "Surely the darkness shall cover me, the light shall be night about me:"

12. Even the darkness is not dark for You; but the night shines like the day; darkness is as light with You:

13. For You have formed my insides; You knit me together in my mother's womb:

14. I will praise You; for I am fearfully and wonderfully made; Marvelous are Your works! And my soul knows that right well:

15. My frame was not hidden from You, when I was made in secret, and finely wrought in the depths of the earth:

טז. גָּלְמִי רָאוּ עֵינֶיךָ, וְעַל־סִפְרְךָ כֻּלָּם יִכָּתֵבוּ, יָמִים יֻצָּרוּ וְלוֹ אֶחָד בָּהֶם: יז. וְלִי מַה־יָּקְרוּ רֵעֶיךָ אֵל, מֶה עָצְמוּ רָאשֵׁיהֶם: יח. אֶסְפְּרֵם מֵחוֹל יִרְבּוּן, הֱקִיצֹתִי וְעוֹדִי עִמָּךְ: יט. אִם־ תִּקְטֹל אֱלוֹהַּ רָשָׁע, וְאַנְשֵׁי דָמִים סוּרוּ מֶנִּי: כ. אֲשֶׁר יֹאמְרֻךָ לִמְזִמָּה, נָשֻׂא לַשָּׁוְא עָרֶיךָ: כא. הֲלוֹא־מְשַׂנְאֶיךָ יְהוָה אֶשְׂנָא, וּבִתְקוֹמְמֶיךָ אֶתְקוֹטָט: כב. תַּכְלִית שִׂנְאָה שְׂנֵאתִים, לְאוֹיְבִים הָיוּ לִי: כג. חָקְרֵנִי אֵל וְדַע לְבָבִי, בְּחָנֵנִי וְדַע שַׂרְעַפָּי: כד. וּרְאֵה אִם־דֶּרֶךְ עֹצֶב בִּי, וּנְחֵנִי בְּדֶרֶךְ עוֹלָם:

16. Your eyes saw my unformed substance; and in Your book all things were written; also the days in which they are to be fashioned,[1] and for it too there was one of them:

17. How precious also are Your thoughts to me, O God! How vast is their sum:

18. If I should count them, they are more in number than the sand; when I awake, I am still with You:

19. Surely You will slay the wicked, O God! Depart from me therefore, you bloody men:

20. For they speak against You wickedly, and Your enemies take Your name in vain:

21. Do I not hate them, Hashem, those who hate You? And do I not strive with those who rise up against You:

22. I hate them with the utmost hatred; I count them my enemies:

23. Search me, O God, and know my heart! Test me, and know my thoughts:

24. And see if there is any wicked way in me, and lead me in the way everlasting:

---

1. *Hashem foresees the future although none of it has yet occurred.*

It is recommended to recite the Section of the Torah dealing with Repentance. One who says this section will merit divine inspiration to repent.

פרשת תשובה

א. וְהָיָה כִי יָבֹאוּ עָלֶיךָ כָּל הַדְּבָרִים הָאֵלֶּה, הַבְּרָכָה וְהַקְּלָלָה אֲשֶׁר נָתַתִּי לְפָנֶיךָ, וַהֲשֵׁבֹתָ אֶל לְבָבֶךָ, בְּכָל הַגּוֹיִם אֲשֶׁר הִדִּיחֲךָ יהוה אֱלֹהֶיךָ שָׁמָּה: ב. וְשַׁבְתָּ עַד יהוה אֱלֹהֶיךָ, וְשָׁמַעְתָּ בְקֹלוֹ, כְּכֹל אֲשֶׁר אָנֹכִי מְצַוְּךָ הַיּוֹם, אַתָּה וּבָנֶיךָ בְּכָל לְבָבְךָ וּבְכָל נַפְשֶׁךָ: ג. וְשָׁב יהוה אֱלֹהֶיךָ אֶת שְׁבוּתְךָ וְרִחֲמֶךָ, וְשָׁב וְקִבֶּצְךָ מִכָּל הָעַמִּים, אֲשֶׁר הֱפִיצְךָ יהוה אֱלֹהֶיךָ שָׁמָּה: ד. אִם יִהְיֶה נִדַּחֲךָ בִּקְצֵה הַשָּׁמָיִם, מִשָּׁם יְקַבֶּצְךָ יהוה אֱלֹהֶיךָ וּמִשָּׁם יִקָּחֶךָ: ה. וֶהֱבִיאֲךָ יהוה אֱלֹהֶיךָ אֶל הָאָרֶץ אֲשֶׁר יָרְשׁוּ אֲבֹתֶיךָ וִירִשְׁתָּהּ, וְהֵיטִבְךָ וְהִרְבְּךָ מֵאֲבֹתֶיךָ: ו. וּמָל יהוה אֱלֹהֶיךָ אֶת לְבָבְךָ וְאֶת לְבַב זַרְעֶךָ, לְאַהֲבָה אֶת יהוה אֱלֹהֶיךָ בְּכָל לְבָבְךָ וּבְכָל נַפְשְׁךָ, לְמַעַן חַיֶּיךָ: ז. וְנָתַן יהוה אֱלֹהֶיךָ אֵת כָּל הָאָלוֹת הָאֵלֶּה, עַל אֹיְבֶיךָ

It is recommended to recite the Section of the Torah dealing with Repentance. One who says this section will merit divine inspiration to repent.

The Section of Teshuvah

1. And it shall come to pass, when all these things have come upon you, the blessing and the curse, which I have set before you, and you shall take it to heart among all the nations, where Hashem, your God has driven you:

2. And you will return to Hashem, your God, and will obey His voice, to all that I command you this day, you and your children, with all your heart, and with all your soul:

3. Then Hashem, your God will return you from captivity, and have compassion upon you, and will return and gather you from among all the nations, where Hashem, your God has scattered you:

4. If your exile has been driven out to the farthest parts of heaven, from there will Hashem, your God gather you, and from there will He fetch you:

5. And Hashem, your God will bring you into the land which your fathers possessed, and you shall possess it; and He will be good to you, and cause you to multiply more than your fathers:

6. And Hashem, your God will circumcise your heart, and the heart of your seed, to love Hashem, your God with all your heart, and with all your soul, in order that you may live:

7. And Hashem, your God will put all these curses upon your enemies, and on those who hate you, who persecuted you:

וְעַל שֹׂנְאֶיךָ אֲשֶׁר רְדָפוּךָ: ח. וְאַתָּה תָשׁוּב,
וְשָׁמַעְתָּ בְּקוֹל יהוה, וְעָשִׂיתָ אֶת כָּל מִצְוֹתָיו
אֲשֶׁר אָנֹכִי מְצַוְּךָ הַיּוֹם. ט. וְהוֹתִירְךָ יהוה
אֱלֹהֶיךָ בְּכֹל מַעֲשֵׂה יָדֶךָ, בִּפְרִי בִטְנְךָ וּבִפְרִי
בְהֶמְתְּךָ וּבִפְרִי אַדְמָתְךָ לְטֹבָה, כִּי יָשׁוּב יהוה
לָשׂוּשׂ עָלֶיךָ לְטוֹב, כַּאֲשֶׁר שָׂשׂ עַל אֲבֹתֶיךָ:
י. כִּי תִשְׁמַע בְּקוֹל יהוה אֱלֹהֶיךָ, לִשְׁמֹר
מִצְוֹתָיו וְחֻקֹּתָיו הַכְּתוּבָה בְּסֵפֶר הַתּוֹרָה
הַזֶּה, כִּי תָשׁוּב אֶל יהוה אֱלֹהֶיךָ בְּכָל לְבָבְךָ
וּבְכָל נַפְשֶׁךָ.

תפילה לאחר פרשת תשובה

יְהִי רָצוֹן מִלְּפָנֶיךָ יהוה אֱלֹהַי וֵאלֹהֵי אֲבוֹתַי, שֶׁתַּחְתּוֹר
חֲתִירָה מִתַּחַת כִּסֵּא כְבוֹדֶךָ, לְהַחֲזִיר בִּתְשׁוּבָה שְׁלֵמָה
לְכָל פּוֹשְׁעֵי עַמְּךָ בֵּית יִשְׂרָאֵל. וּבִכְלָלָם תַּחֲזִירֵנִי בִּתְשׁוּבָה
שְׁלֵמָה לְפָנֶיךָ, כִּי יְמִינְךָ פְּשׁוּטָה לְקַבֵּל שָׁבִים, וְרוֹצֶה
אַתָּה בִּתְשׁוּבָה אָמֵן סֶלָה.

8.   And you shall repent and obey the voice of Hashem, and do all his commandments which I command you this day:

9.   And Hashem, your God will make you abundantly prosperous in every work of your hand, in the fruit of your body, and in the fruit of your cattle, and in the fruit of your land, for good; for Hashem, will again rejoice over your good, as he rejoiced over your fathers:

10.   If you shall listen to the voice of Hashem, your God, to keep his commandments and his statutes which are written in this book of the Torah, and if you return to Hashem, your God with all your heart, and with all your soul:

Prayer After Section of Teshuvah

May it be the will before You, Hashem, my God and the God of my forefathers, that you dig a tunnel beneath Your Throne of glory, to bring back in complete repentance all the sinners of Your nation the household of Israel. And among them return me with complete repentance before You because Your right hand is extended to accept those who return and You desire repentance Amen, Selah.

תפילה על תשובה לרבינו יונה

אָנָּא הַשֵּׁם, חָטָאתִי, עָוִיתִי, פָּשַׁעְתִּי, וְכָזֹאת וְכָזֹאת עָשִׂיתִי
מִיּוֹם הֱיוֹתִי עַל הָאֲדָמָה עַד הַיּוֹם הַזֶּה. וְעַתָּה נְשָׂאַנִי לִבִּי
וְנָדְבָה אוֹתִי רוּחִי לָשׁוּב אֵלֶיךָ בֶּאֱמֶת וּבְלֵב טוֹב וְשָׁלֵם,
בְּכָל לֵב וָנֶפֶשׁ וּמְאֹד, וְלִהְיוֹת מוֹדֶה וְעוֹזֵב וּלְהַשְׁלִיךְ
מֵעָלַי כָּל פְּשָׁעַי, וְלַעֲשׂוֹת לִי לֵב חָדָשׁ וְרוּחַ חֲדָשָׁה,
וְלִהְיוֹת זָרִיז וְזָהִיר בְּיִרְאָתֶךָ. וְעַתָּה ה' אֱלֹהַי, הַפּוֹתֵחַ יָד
בִּתְשׁוּבָה וּמְסַיֵּעַ לַבָּאִים לִטַּהֵר, פְּתַח יָדְךָ וְקַבְּלֵנִי
בִּתְשׁוּבָה שְׁלֵמָה לְפָנֶיךָ, וְסַיְּעֵנִי לְהִתְחַזֵּק בְּיִרְאָתֶךָ, וְעָזְרֵנִי
נֶגֶד הַשָּׂטָן הַנִּלְחָם בִּי בְּתַחְבּוּלוֹת תָּמִיד וּמְבַקֵּשׁ נַפְשִׁי
לַהֲמִיתֵנִי, לְבִלְתִּי יִמְשָׁל בִּי, וְתַרְחִיקֵהוּ מֵרַמַ"ח אֵבָרִים
שֶׁבִּי וְתַשְׁלִיכֵהוּ בִּמְצֻלוֹת יָם, וְתִגְעַר בּוֹ לְבִלְתִּי יַעֲמֹד עַל
יְמִינִי לְשִׂטְנִי, וְעָשִׂיתָ אֶת אֲשֶׁר אֵלֵךְ בְּחֻקֶּיךָ, וַהֲסִירוֹת לֵב
הָאֶבֶן מִקִּרְבִּי וְנָתַתָּ לִי לֵב בָּשָׂר. אָנָּא ה' אֱלֹהַי, שְׁמַע אֶל
תְּפִלַּת עַבְדְּךָ וְאֶל תַּחֲנוּנָיו וְקַבֵּל תְּשׁוּבָתִי, וְאַל יְעַכֵּב שׁוּם
חֵטְא וְעָוֹן אֶת תְּפִלָּתִי וּתְשׁוּבָתִי, וְיִהְיוּ לִפְנֵי כִסֵּא כְבוֹדְךָ
מְלִיצֵי יֹשֶׁר לְהָלִיץ בַּעֲדִי לְהַכְנִיס תְּפִלָּתִי לְפָנֶיךָ. וְאִם
בַּחֲטָאַי הָרַב וְעָצוּם אֵין לִי מֵלִיץ יֹשֶׁר, חֲתֹר לִי אַתָּה
מִתַּחַת כִּסֵּא כְבוֹדְךָ וְקַבֵּל תְּשׁוּבָתִי, וְלֹא אָשׁוּב רֵיקָם
מִלְּפָנֶיךָ, כִּי אַתָּה שׁוֹמֵעַ תְּפִלָּה.

Prayer for Repentance

I beg of You Hashem, I have transgressed, sinned and rebelled, from the day I was placed on the earth until this day, now my heart has uplifted me and my spirit has ennobled me to return to You truthfully, with a complete and sincere heart, with all my heart, soul and being. I acknowledge and forsake my sins and I accept to make for myself a new heart and spirit. I will be careful and quick to fear You. And now, Hashem, my God, Who opens His hand to those who repent and helps those who come to purify, open Your hand and accept me with complete repentance before You. Help me to be strong in Your service and protect me from Satan who fights with tricky against me and wants to destroy my soul. Do not let him rule over me, and keep him far from my 248 limbs and cast him to the depths of the sea and denounce him so that he not stand at my right side to lead me astray. You should cause me to follow in Your statutes and You shall remove the heart of stone from within me and You shall give to me a heart of flesh. I beg Hashem, my God, listen to the prayer of Your servant and to his supplication and accept my repentance. Let no sin or transgression hold back my prayer and repentance. Let there be before Your Throne of glory, angels of defense to defend on my behalf to bring my prayer before You. And if with my great and many sins I have no one to take my defense; You, tunnel beneath Your Throne of glory and accept my repentance. Do not turn me away empty-handed from before You, because You listen to prayer.